Before The Ending

Of The Day

Norman Pittenger

MOREHOUSE-BARLOW

WILTON, CT

i

Morehouse Barlow Co., Inc.
78 Danbury Road
Wilton, Connecticut 06897

ISBN 0-8192-1362-4

Library of Congress Catalog Card Number 84-62373

Printed in the United States of America

Contents

A Prefatory Note

v

A Prefatory Note

The title of this small book, "Before the Ending of the Day," is open to two possible interpretations.

The first of them will be obvious to anybody who is familiar with the lovely "evening office" of Compline, originally used in monasteries and convents but now popular with laypeople of all denominations as well. It comes from the first words of the prescribed hymn for Compline: "Before the ending of the day, Creator of the world, we pray that with thy wonted favour thou wouldst be our guard and keeper now." The hymn is sung as part of the preparation for a night of rest. It asks that those who (in other words from Compline) are "wearied by the changes of this fleeting world" may be enabled to find their true security in God's "eternal changelessness"—which does not mean some imagined portrayal of deity as unrelated, immutable, impassive, but rather the divine faithfulness in love and care for God's creation and especially for God's human children.

Hence one possible interpretation is simply *evening,* in the simple sense of the word. But there is another possible understanding too. It is suggested by the phrase in which St. John of the Cross, the austere yet immensely attractive Spanish mystic of the sixteenth century, says that "in the evening of our day, we shall be judged by our loving." That is, the reference is not to the termination of a twenty-four hour worldly day. Rather, it is a reference to the ending of human mortal existence for each of us. Night-time serves as an appropriate symbol for what an old German chorale calls the moment before "death's dark night" comes to humankind.

These then are the two possible meanings; and in this book I shall consider both of them. For me this seems a proper thing to do, since I have now reached and passed four-score years of human life.

Every day comes to its end and I sleep in the hope that on the morrow I may awake to another day's responsibilities and delights. But every day is also for me—and even for the youngest of my readers too—something else. It is a nearer approach to death. And before the ending of day in *that* sense, I (and everybody) must prepare myself, so far as I am able, to face the inescapable fact that there will be the writing of a *finis*, "the end," on the last page of the last chapter of the book of my mortal life. Like taxes, as the saying goes, death is unavoidable; and the wise man or woman, certainly the Christian man or woman, must always remember this.

I have gathered together here bits and pieces of meditative writing which I have put on paper over a decade or so. This material is given such unity as it may have by the concern which I have to give to life's termination as this is symbolized by "the ending of the day" in clock-time. I have sought to avoid discussing this in "purple-passages," since I am always a little uncomfortable when I find them in what I happen to be reading. I have tried to speak simply and directly about the subject, in the hope that what is being said will be helpful to others, young or old, as they in their turn come to sense the fleeting nature of human existence; and, having grasped this, have sought to do what an uncle of mine (then in his seventies) once called "making a treaty of peace with the inexorable reality of things." Most of what is here written has been suggested to me by a consideration of various phrases from parts of the Compline office.

Which brings me to my final remark in this prefatory note. During a long life I have been continually in what might be styled a somewhat ambiguous position. On the one hand, I have been both attracted and enriched by a love for, as well as a regular participation in, the splendid liturgical life of the Christian Church. For me this has been "Catholic spirituality" as expressed in the inherited liturgical tradition. On the other hand, I have been discontented, indeed unhappy, at the way in which the deepest insight and affirmation of the living tradition which *is* Christianity are stated in idioms and concepts that have little direct relation to what modern men and women know and think about themselves and their world. Much has been put in a way that bears little relation to that deepest insight and affirmation. This has distressed me to such a degree that I have devoted most of my life, when not engaged in the teaching which has been my vocation, to the endeavour to find an appropriate conceptuality for Christian faith and then a way to employ that conceptuality to state what Christian reality is all about. My concern here has been to help our contemporaries understand, and accept with all their heart and soul and mind, that reality.

Something of the ambiguity of the title will certainly appear in these pages. I am not ashamed that this is so. In any event, it cannot be avoided if I am to be honest with my readers. My earnest desire is that what is said here will be helpful to such readers, even if now and again I may seem to build positive statements on what might appear to be negative views.

The service of Compline, as set forth in the American Book of Common Prayer 1979, is printed as an appendix to this book. It is found on pages 127 to 135 of that Prayer Book. Readers may wish to refer to it from time to time; and some, I trust, will make the use of that service part of their Christian devotions.

Norman Pittenger

King's College
Cambridge, England

I

A Peaceful Night and a Perfect End

We have done a hard day's work, whatever our job may happen to be; and when the evening comes and we are preparing to go to bed for the night, we usually hope that we shall have a quiet and peaceful rest. We do not wish to retire for the night in a condition of mental confusion, with minds troubled and hearts uneasy. If we go to bed in that state, we shall probably not sleep very well; if we sleep at all our sleep will be unquiet and we shall probably awaken again and again. Maybe we shall even find ourselves possessed by what Henry David Thoreau so well described as a condition of "quiet desperation," from which there may be little if any escape.

This is why so many of our friends these days swallow some sedative, of greater or less strength, to ensure that they shall be able to sleep through the night and awaken in the morning—a little groggy perhaps—but prepared to face the duties of another day as best they can.

Over the years it has often struck me that it is not only older persons like myself who may find such sedation necessary. Younger men and women seem increasingly prone to its use. They do not wish, maybe they do not dare, to trust themselves to the natural capacity of body and mind to guarantee a "good night's rest," as they might phrase it. Indeed we are informed by those supposed to know that the use of various kinds of sedatives by young people has grown enormously in our own time. Some of these experts look upon this as a disturbing fact which does not augur well for the human race.

Artificial inducement of repose can be a dangerous thing in the long run, they say. However all this may be, Christian men and women ought to be among those who have quietened their minds and spirits in such a fashion that artificial means are not required to give them a peaceful night.

And the rest of the phrase from the Compline office, with which this chapter concerns itself, must not be forgotten either. Not only is it "a peaceful night" that is desired by humankind. It is also, even more importantly, "a perfect end." They want to have some way in which when "life's fitful fever" is over, they can come to death in the confidence that there is an end, a goal, a meaning, which redeems it from sheer futility and provides an assurance that their existence, whether it be long or short in terms of years, is truly significant. They want it to have a genuine value, not merely to be the conclusion of "a tale, told by an idiot, full of sound and fury, signifying nothing." Probably it is only the older of us who will feel this acutely. Younger people have so many present interests and so much which engages their attention that they can and usually do neglect matters of this sort. As the saying goes, "Well, tomorrow is another day!" The older of us cannot say this. Maybe tomorrow will *not* be "another day," but will never come at all. Our mortal existence will have reached its end— and there is nothing that we can do about it, beyond accepting the fact for what it is: inevitable, inescapable, entirely certain. We are going to die; there is no doubt about it. Hence for some of us at least there is the question, "How can we have confidence that there is for us 'a perfect end'?" And if there is one, what are we able to say about it, with as much integrity of mind as we can muster?

Just here we come to one central aspect of a genuine Christian faith. It is by no means the whole of that faith; neither is it likely to be very meaningful if we separate it from other aspects, since its validity depends largely on them. In a strange way, the desire for some such assurance is like the wish to sleep well after a busy day's activity. Hence it is natural for the two notions to be linked together as they are in the words from Compline. One of the Psalms says that God "gives his beloved sleep." We pray that this may be true for us each night: a refreshing period of slumber which prepares us for still another day of effort. In what sense, in what way if any, does God stand ready to give those who are thus "beloved" the confidence to face death with equanimity and to make the moment of dying as "perfect" as they want it to be?

Let us think a bit about this question and try to see what the faith which Christians hold has to say to us here.

I think that I am not speaking inaccurately when I say that for vast numbers of people, very likely brought up within some version of Christian allegiance, most of the old ways of answering do not seem available today. There was a time, not so long ago, when our wider culture took more or less for granted a picture of the world, which permitted an acceptance of the idea that at the moment of death humans entered upon another mode of life in a state or situation called "heaven." The sort of existence we know in *this* world would be renewed, with appropriate differences, in *another* world. I remember that when I was a very young child and a dearly beloved older sister died, I was told by an uncle who sought to console me that she had "gone to heaven." There she was now wonderfully happy and there all pain and suffering, all problems and difficulties, were resolved or absent. I wondered what this could mean and in my childish way asked about it. The reply was given, without hesitation, that to be "in heaven" meant to be alive, completely conscious of being alive, existing just as one had done here and now, save that "heaven" included my sister's being quite wonderfully aware of God as her loving heavenly Father and aware of me too. So I need not mourn nor feel any sadness about her leaving me; she was still as much herself as she had ever been, with all the characteristics that I had known and cared for.

The picture of what happens at death with which I was there presented made it like going into another room in the same house. Everything would be the same excepting the obvious fact that it was *another* room, not the one in which I had my own little existence. So dying became an incidental matter. I was told that all of us who were Christians believed in this way. Of course our present human body did not persist but what was really *me* and what was really my beloved *sister* was something called "a soul," whose nature was not discussed but which was said to be the true and abiding self which I knew and which I knew also in the case of that sister.

As I have said, I suspect that a great many of us today find this sort of talk pretty difficult if not entirely impossible. I suspect also that there are millions of people who in word may accept it, perhaps even believe that they do accept it; yet in truth it cuts no ice with them. To all intents and purposes they find it no real part of their sure conviction. At best it is a wistful idea which they may *want* to have vital in their thinking but which somehow fails to become compelling to them.

That we die is plainly a fact. But what it entails is not at all clear. So we are likely to settle for our present finite existence in this world; and only when someone we care for comes to die or when we ourselves know that our own death is approaching and become aware that we are indeed near "the ending of the day" do we bother much about it. "One world at a time," so to say.

Yet if the basic faith of the Christian tradition is in any real fashion the truth, opening to us a deeper awareness of how things go in the world, something must be affirmed which speaks to the question of human dying.

As we go on in our meditations drawn from words in Compline, we shall have a good deal to say about what I have called "the basic faith of the Christian tradition." Here I shall not anticipate that consideration; but I must indicate one, and that one the primary, point with which this faith is concerned. Put very simply, it is this: in the event in human history which we indicate when we say "Jesus Christ," there is a disclosure in concrete fact of something whose importance cannot be denied. That disclosure can be stated in a few words, although its implication and application would require long exposition. The conviction of the Christian tradition is that the "whatever-it-is" which is creative, life-enhancing as well as life-giving, which is supremely worshipful, entirely dependable, utterly trustworthy, supreme above all else, is a Love, a divine Lover, from whom all comes, to whom all goes. This being has, in that historical event, so acted that its (or his, or her) character is known to be precisely such Love. From a response to that originative event, says the Christian tradition, we grasp dimly but surely that we are made by Love, for Love, in Love—a Love that "moves the sun and the other stars," as Dante put it in the very last words of *The Divine Comedy*. Above all, we grasp dimly but surely that this same Love can and does *move us humans*. From that Love we come; to that Love we go. Such is the primary assertion of Christian faith. It is not demonstrable but it is not unreasonable. What is significant for us when we think about "the ending of our day" is its relevance to human destiny.

The consequences of this central affirmation can be and have been worked out in various ways. One of those ways has been the set of beliefs which I was taught as a child and with which my uncle sought to console me when my sister died. There may be another way, however, which speaks more directly and credibly to us today. I am sure that there is; and in the rest of this opening chapter I shall present it for the reader's consideration.

We are aware that we all live in a world where relationships are both desirable and given. None of us lives to and for and by and with self alone. There is a give-and-take about our existence which is inescapable; what is more, it is precisely this give-and-take which offers us delight and gives us sadness. May it not be that the whole creation is like that too? It may be a creation in which relationships are at the heart of the enterprise. And if there be God, that Love and Lover about whom I have just spoken, must not God too be involved in relationships?

Much in our inherited thinking about God has made deity so *in*dependent, so utterly self-contained or self-subsistent, so unaffected by the world that he or she or it does not experience such relationship. For after all, to be related to something is to be affected and influenced by it. Above all, to love is to be thus affected or influenced, with the joy and the pain that are always present in loving. I think that we should say this about God, although at the same time we must also say that the divine existence *as such* is not dependent for its existence on whatever it is with whom God is so intimately related. On the other hand, what happens to others also happens in cosmic Love. Love *cares*, to the point of sharing in those others' existence in the most real fashion.

If God is affected in this way, through sharing with the world and with us who are in the world and are part of the world, can we not make bold to say that this divine Lover accepts us into the life which is divine—welcomes, receives and makes a continuing fact in the divine experience, the existence which is our own?

Now this does not carry with it the necessary implication that after death we are just as we were before death. Death makes a difference. It puts the word *finis* to our mortal life here and now in a created world. Yet that word *finis* may not be the very last word.

For it could be—and I am convinced that it is so—that our continuing in the life of God is a necessary consequence of our having existed at all. To put it in another way, we are unfailingly *remembered* in God, whose memory includes whatever has been accomplished for good and who remembers also whatever good may be brought out of what has been evil or false or untrue or wrong.

It may be that thus to be "remembered" by God carries with it the possibility of a conscious awareness of selfhood. That is not a total impossibility, although I think that it is by no means a necessary part of the picture. However it may be, to be received into the divine life is no negation of what value or significance we may have had in the "big picture;" it is only a way of affirming that such value and significance is never denied and cannot be lost. It is safe forever in the divine life, "where moth and rust do not consume or destroy."

For me, and maybe for others, such considerations help to make possible for us, at the moment of our death, "a perfect end." For surely nothing could be better than to be in God who *is* the perfect Lover.

It has been unfortunate that a good deal of talk on these matters has seemed so often to think of our human destiny as something other than this. Rewards of some kind, "heavenly pleasures," even what St. Francis de Sales called "the consolations of God," have been put in the primary position. But genuine Christian faith ought to see that *God* is our human destiny and that to be taken into the divine life is the "perfect end" for all our human living and endeavour.

To have such a conviction as the deepest reality of our human existence is to be delivered from fuss and worry about our little selves. It is to have humility instead of pride as the appropriate human attitude or posture. What is more, it is to be able to go to sleep at night, at "the ending of our day" in the temporal sense, without anxious concern about what is to happen next day or spending our time and our attention worrying about what we have been doing during the daylight "before the ending of the day." A prayer in the old American Book of Common Prayer speaks of "the fears and anxieties" which so bother us and so interfere with our living with a measure of serenity and acceptance. But to know that we are held in the hands of an unshakeable Love, from which our tiny existence came and to which in the end it is to go, can provide the stability that we need if we are not constantly to be tossed about by the changing fashions of the world in which we live. That we should be deeply concerned for and about that world is obvious; we should be less than human, more "like the beasts that perish," did we not have such concern. But that is different from deep anxiety.

When I go to bed at night, I am permitted—if this Christian conviction possesses me—to commit myself to a loving Creator who is also a loving deliverer from fears, worries, bothers, and anxieties. Thus I pray that I shall have "a peaceful night" quite as much as "a perfect end." Somehow the two go together. The way to both is in being ready "before the ending of the day" in both senses of that phrase, to say in the words also in the Compline office, "Unto you, O God, I commit myself"—for every moment of this present life and for what will happen when I come, as come I must, to the time of my death.

In a way it is astonishing, yet it is a fact, that an Englishwoman, a recluse who spent half-a-century in a cell attached to a church in Norwich, seems often to have penetrated more deeply into the realities of Christian faith than those who are much better known and more frequently quoted. I am referring to Mother Julian of Norwich whose dates are approximately 1342 to 1412. A book which she wrote during those years in her cell is called *Shewings* (or *Revelations*) *of Divine Love*. In that book she recounts a series of disclosures, made through some sort of vision, in which she came to understand with extraordinary clarity who God is, what God wills, and what God does in the world and for God's human children. There are many passages which might be quoted but one is especially relevant to our present concern. Here it is: "Peace and love are always alive in us but we are not always alive to peace and love." This she could say because she said also, in the same writing, that she had been enabled to see that "the sweet eye of [God's] pity is never turned from us, and the operation of [God's] mercy does not cease." Always, even when we fall into error and into sin, as also during our moments of worry and fear, of unquiet and wrong, God's pity and mercy are present. For Mother Julian that fact is the very basis of human existence, just as God is also "the ground" of "all our beseeching" or praying.

Mother Julian boldly declared that God always "looks upon us with pity and not with blame" because God, whom she spoke about in her own fascinating way as both our Father *and* our Mother, *is* Love. God is inescapable, so that even when we presume to deny God we can do so only because we are sustained by the divine loving.

Now it is possible, of course, to sentimentalize this portrayal of God—and to do that is a temptation to which many of us are prone, once we have reacted against the imperialist, patriarchal, tyrannical, and demandingly moralistic pictures found so often in conventional Christian teaching and preaching and liturgical worship. Mother Julian *never* sentimentalized. Anybody who reads her book can see clearly that she was a woman who faced things as they were and refused altogether to adopt a sloppy and easy way of describing deity. For her the very strength and power of God were discovered in the divine pity and compassion, the divine loving and caring. Our all-too-human reading of strength and power in terms of coercive action and sheer exercise of force is just wrong—so Julian told us.

Precisely because God is not only like that but *is* that—the divine worshipful, dependable reality named "infinite Love," because in the event of Jesus Christ "pure unbounded Love" (as Charles Wesley's hymn puts it) was enacted and released humanly—precisely because this *is* the case, no human can be utterly hopeless or entirely helpless. Into God's hands we can dare to commit ourselves. As Mother Julian writes, in her famous lines quoted by T. S. Eliot in *Four Quartets,* "all shall be well, and all shall be well, and all manner of thing shall be well"—not by denying or forgetting the inquietude we know so well, like the worries and perplexities and uncertainties which can make our nights restless and prevent our getting the sleep we need, but rather by triumphing in love through and in spite of all these human negativities.

The Compline office is intended to prepare us, "before the ending of the day," for "a peaceful night and a perfect end." Those who through the years have come to value that office will testify that its recitation can and does do just that. So far we have looked at only one phrase found in the service. In the chapters which follow we shall look at others, all of which have the same over-arching purpose. As the office itself says, "I will lay me down in peace and take my rest, for it is you Lord only who makes me dwell in safety."

II

The Grace and Comfort of the Holy Spirit

Not by our own efforts but only by reliance on the loving action of God in us and for us can we be enabled to know peaceful nights and to have a "perfect end." Hence in Compline we pray that we may receive "the *grace* and *comfort* of the *Holy Spirit*." I wish to make several points about that phrase; I have italicized in quoting it the words which modern logical analysts would style "operational." Each of them is of very great importance and should be understood by all of us.

In the first place *grace* has often been wrongly interpreted in Christian thinking and this mistake has had serious consequences for Christian life and spirituality. The error is to be seen, for instance, in the familiar words of the collect for the Annunciation in older Prayer Books of the Anglican communion, in which we ask that grace be "poured" into our hearts. It is as if grace were some *thing* or commodity; whereas it is always a matter of personal relationships which cannot be described properly in "thing language." Again, grace has very frequently, indeed almost universally, been seen as separate from and less than God. In Cardinal Newman's familiar hymn from *The Dream of Gerontius*, we are told that "a higher gift than grace" is "God's presence and his very self and essence all-divine." This is totally false. As the Oxford theologian N. P. Williams demonstrated decades ago, with evidence from Scripture to back his argument, grace *is* God's very self, the "essence all-divine" which is deity. It is nothing other and nothing less than *God in loving activity*, not something added onto or working for God.

In the second place, grace is to be seen as a freely given gift of God. We can never earn it, we can never deserve it. As theologians have said, it is "gratuitous." This is a blow to our human pride and self-will; all too much of the time we think that we can so act that God is compelled to show loving favour and act graciously towards us. But the contrary is the case. *Because* God surrounds us with grace and *because* this is prior to any initiative of human responsiveness, we are led to do the right things. This is the point of the doctrine of "justification (being put right with God) through divine grace and by human faith," (recovered during the Reformation in the sixteenth century). Martin Luther did not invent this; he found it in the New Testament—and *all* Christians, including those who speak for the Roman Catholic Church, acknowledge this today.

In the third place, the common definitions of grace are far too precise and complicated. There has been talk about habitual grace, actual grace, sacramental grace, prevenient grace, concomitant grace, grace of perseverance, and in Reformed circles "indefectible grace." When we make these artificial distinctions, the whole enterprise looks like a shopping list of possible goods to be acquired. What we ought to have seen is that God's loving activity—Bishop Kenneth Kirk spoke well of grace as "God's love in action" which (if we have the correct thought about God) must mean *God* in loving action—is constantly present. "A thing *is* what it *does*," said Alfred North Whitehead, discussing the natural order; that must be said also about animate matter, human existence, and even about God. God *is* what God *does*. It is not only God's "property," as a Prayer Book collect phrases it, it is also and primarily God's *nature*, "to have mercy and to forgive." That is what God is. Hence all divine working, all divine presentness, is gracious. It is all grace.

Finally, grace is not shown only to divine favorites; it is "promiscuous," as we might dare to put it. The traditional teaching about "election," found of course in the Pauline epistles, must surely be interpreted in the universalist manner Karl Barth suggested, not in the highly selective manner about which many Calvinist theologians have talked. Their gloomy view of human nature had its point, to be sure, since everything that we men and women think or say or do is somehow "tainted" with self-will and self-seeking. Their insistence on the truth that many if not most people do not seem to have shown the "fruit" of grace led them astray, however, bringing them to think that God's action towards humans has a "preferential quality," giving grace to some and withholding it from others. Surely Barth was correct when he says that God elects *all* humankind; and that even Jesus Christ, understood as "the Elect Man," is chosen by God for the sole purpose of effecting a gracious relationship for that total humanity in which his life took part.

So much about grace. My second word is *comfort*. Far too much of the time we understand "comfort" as if it were cosiness and ease, and the sort of thing that we indicate today when we speak of somebody's being "comfortable" or happily and pleasantly at rest. But the very word, in its Latin derivation, says something different. *Con-fortis* means a strengthening, invigorating, refreshing, and renewing presence with us on the part of some other who is able to provide just this sort of empowering. So to pray for "the comfort of the Holy Spirit" is not to ask that we shall be "at east in Sion;" rather, it is to ask that God, through the Holy Spirit, shall work in us and upon us in a fashion that will strengthen us for living obediently and faithfully in any and every human situation.

As to the words *Holy Spirit,* what is there being indicated is the divine responsivity operative throughout the creation. In the terms of traditional triunitarian thought, God is the creative source ("the Father"); God is the expressive act ("the Word" or "the Son"); and God is the vivifying, enabling activity which is present throughout creation and which "answers back" as a great *Amen* to that which God has expressed and done in the world. Yet it is all *one God* in differing modes of the divine selfhood.

What has been said so far in this chapter may seem to some to be abstract theologizing. On the contrary, it is directly and immediately relevant to every aspect of Christian experience, above all to our "life in grace" and to our spirituality. Surely I need not indicate at length how each of my points has its significance in these respects. But very briefly, it is simply saying that in our asking for "the grace and comfort of the Holy Spirit" we are in truth desiring with all our hearts that we shall be conformed to God's living will, share in God's loving purposes, and respond to God's loving care for us—and thus be ready, at "the ending of the day," to "take our rest" in the assurance that we *are* "cared for." So we may sleep in peace; and when our death comes, as come it will sooner or later, we may also be ready to commit ourselves, in the wholeness of our human existence, to the divine Love "which will not let us go."

In the life lived in communion with Christ, we are not delivered from all anxieties and worries. And we have to learn that there is indeed (as the Old Testament book of Ecclesiastes reminds us) "a time to weep and a time to laugh." Nobody can escape this. In a strange way joy and sorrow are intermingled in our experience. If we are to have "peace in believing," we need to see that "the grace and comfort of the Holy Spirit" will give us the courage to accept every situation as it comes. Reinhold Niebuhr, the great American theologian of the last generation, once wrote a prayer in which he asked that we should understand both what can be changed and what cannot be changed, with "the wisdom to know the difference." One of the things that cannot be changed is this combination of laughter and weeping in our human existence. A great deal depends here, of course, on how we see these two; and those of us who dare to call ourselves Christian have something important to contribute at this point.

But first of all we must grasp the patent fact that no responsible Christian, however much he or she is aware of the grace and comfort that come from God, can be a complete optimist. Neither can a Christian be a complete pessimist. We are to be realistic as we look at ourselves, our fellow-humans, the world, and what happens in it. Hence we shall not deny the anguish nor exaggerate the joy. We must attempt to see things "steadily and see them whole," as Matthew Arnold once phrased it. If there is a sense in which Christians, knowing the Spirit's gift of grace and comfort, know that *joy* is the last word, it is also true that we dare not be blind to the pain which is so dreadfully real in this world.

The poet John Masefield once wrote that "the days that make us happy are the days that make us wise." He was wrong. It is much more accurate to say that "the days which make us sorrowful are the days that make us wise." This does not require us to *invite* suffering; on the contrary we should do all that is possible to ameliorate whatever anguish is known to humankind. But for Jesus himself, as the Letter to the Hebrews tells us, there was a "suffering" through which he "learned" God's will and way for him. The Greek word translated "suffer" has a double meaning: endurance of pain *and* ordinary experience as we know it. No faithful Christian will wish it otherwise for herself or himself.

For Jesus, then, there was "a time to weep" *and* "a time to laugh." All human life is like that; and even the Son of Man, intimately at one with his heavenly Father, was not spared the weeping—indeed we read in the Fourth Gospel about one incident of his weeping, although we also can see that he knew an abiding happiness. "The Captain of our salvation" was like us in this, as in all else save sin. That is what we mean when we say that he was genuinely human.

I want to urge that in God too there is the experience of joy and of sorrow. God, the personalized reality who is utterly dependable, entirely worshipful, and unsurpassed by anything that is not himself (herself), is for Christian faith sheer Love-in-act. And love always shares in sorrow and in joy, if it is not reduced to mere sentimentality. Of course it is not conventional to speak in this fashion about God; in our Christian tradition the stress has been so much on the divine joy that the divine anguish has been overlooked by a great many in that tradition. But if God cannot share both in sorrow *and* in joy, then God is not truly perfect—for, as we shall say again in a later chapter, the true meaning of "perfection" is not absolute immutability and impassibility, but rather a capacity to participate in the lives of the ones who are loved and hence to experience most profoundly their joys and their sorrows. God is like that; that is what calling God "loving" amounts to if we take it with utmost seriousness and not merely an adjective modifying (but not very much) the traditional phrase "unchangeable substance."

"The brief Galilean vision" of God, as Whitehead phrased it, makes all this quite plain to us. The divine joy is most profoundly there, but it is not a denial of pain; rather, it is the overcoming of or the triumph over pain in all its forms. The truth is that to love *is* to suffer. That is why we use the word "passion" rather than a less strong and colorful word. Even in the ecstasy of our human loving, there is a touch of sadness—sadness that our loving is so limited; sadness that there are separations; sadness because of the "unplumbed, salt, estranging sea" (another phrase of Matthew Arnold's) which makes it impossible for anybody to be wholly and fully one with the beloved; sadness because of love's necessary renunciation of self; sadness that lovers must part . . . and we could go on with that listing. Even to live at all is always to "die a little every day;" although the Christian is confident that there can be joy in a newness of life through God's grace and through the comfort (or strengthing and refreshing) which is the gift of God's Holy Spirit.

Some of us are temperamentally more on the optimistic side; others more on the pessimistic side. My plea here is that we should learn to be realistic, so far as we are able, coming to see that joy and sorrow are intermingled, not wanting to be delivered from one so that we can know only the other. But the final end or goal, in Christian faith, is a sharing in the joy which is God. As enacted in the event of Jesus Christ, God is disclosed as having experienced the worst of human anguish and through that worst to have come to fulfillment in joy: "who for the joy that was set before him endured the Cross," says Hebrews once again, in speaking of Jesus. *Now* he is "set down at the throne of the majesty on high." What Jesus enacted is what God *is*.

Finally we might well remember that one of Charles Wesley's great hymns is bold enough to assert that the *risen* Lord still bears "those dear tokens of his passion." In other words, the One who has gone before, the One who would bring *us* to the place where he has gone, is not "untouched by the feeling of our infirmities." Rather, he knew— and God knows, if God is genuinely enacted in the manhood of Jesus —the depths as well as the heights of human existence in all their variety and richness. So God is our companion and our continual refreshment, as God is also our primal source and final end.

In gladly receiving "the grace and comfort of the Holy Spirit," given to us by God as his great and inestimable gift for our human wholeness, we are brought to a deeper grasp of what human life is all about, quite as much as a more profound awareness of what *God* is all about. This is why we can say, with the Apostle Paul, "Thanks be to God for his unspeakable gift," the gift which enables us to go on bravely in following the blessed steps of Christ's most holy life.

In the following chapter entitled "Called by Your Name" we shall look at the difference which Christian faith in Jesus Christ, and through him in God, makes in our project for human existence. At the moment I wish to call attention to a related concern, one frequently forgotten I fear, which is directly significant for us in our thinking about God's provision of grace and strength.

While there is indeed a specifically Christian way of seeing this, there is also a more extended and inclusive aspect too. It came to my mind while preparing the present chapter and it was suggested by a passage in The Acts of the Apostles which happened to be one of the appointed readings in the Church of England's listing of appropriate pieces of Scripture. Here is the passage: "And the barbarians showed us no little kindness, for they kindled a fire and received us every one, because it was raining and because it was cold" (Acts 28:12). St. Paul and his companions on their way from Palestine to Rome were shipwrecked off the island of Malta. There they were given a surprising welcome, described in the words which I have quoted. There are several things which may be noticed in this account.

First we must recall that the people whom St. Paul encountered on Malta are called "barbarians." That was the term used by Greeks of the time for those who were untouched by Hellenistic culture. Obviously this was true of the inhabitants of that place. It was also the case that while Malta was included within the confines of the Roman Empire, such historical evidence as we possess indicates that Rome did not bother very much about those who lived there. We notice also that while doubtless these people had a religion of some sort—and archaeological research has shown that it was of a primitive variety—they knew nothing of Jewish faith and certainly had never heard of Jahweh, the God whom the Jewish race worshipped.

Here were people who were not highly civilized, who lived on the fringe of the Roman world, and whose religion, such as it was, possessed no trace of the high ethical monotheism so central to Jewish existence. And of course the faith of Paul, disciple of Christ and proclaimer of God as revealed and at work in him, was entirely unknown to them.

And yet, and yet . . . these same people showed "no little kindness." They took in the shipwrecked passengers; they kindled a fire to give them warmth and comfort. Why? The answer to that question brings us to the second significant point, not spelled out in the passage I have quoted but surely implicit in it. The barbarian people of Malta did what they did for one reason only, so far as we can gather. They saw men in need; they saw them hungry and cold; they saw them in the tragic situation of shipwreck. And they were moved by compassion to do what they could to help.

15

Thus I wish to urge that very often those who do not share our, or perhaps any, faith can in concrete fact manifest something of the compassion of God, "the grace and comfort of the Holy Spirit," although they could not give it that description. There is "that of God," as the Quakers like to say, which is so deep in the human heart that it must express itself when the occasion demands it. Hence we can say that wherever there is a response to human need, a concern for justice among and between men and nations, and the opportunity to "do good," there often is precisely such an expression of what we usually style common decency and a common readiness to give the needed assistance or support.

I am not saying that men and women are all of them fine people who need only a bit more education and a little inspiration to become perfect. Far from it. Whether we like it or not, honesty compels us to see that humans are sinful people, who want their own way most of the time, who can be cruel and ruthless and nasty, and who do not automatically show virtue. There was once a kind of religious liberalism which talked in that cheerful fashion about human beings. Nobody is likely to subscribe to it now. When an American writer said that "what we need is more clarity in thought and less stupidity of mind," somebody responded with the remark, "It is not clarity which we need but charity; it is not overcoming our stupidity which we need but overcoming our cupidity." Lack of charity is all too often present with us; cupidity is all too often a controlling factor in our lives. And we humans are not "sufficient of ourselves to help ourselves." We must have something more than human information and inspiration if we are to become the kind of people we ought to be, the kind of people whom God purposes us to be. That is why the gospel message, with its proclamation of "the Love of God shed abroad in our hearts," is the only answer adequate to our human condition and situation.

And yet again . . . let us not forget that there is a working of God hidden in every human life. Of that working the barbarian people of Malta may stand as a symbol. Even in the worst of us—even in you and me—there is some trace of the divine compassion, some genuine activity of God, some "grace and comfort" given by God's Holy Spirit. In God "we live and move and have our being," even if we do not always recognize this to be the case. Our grateful acceptance of this truth, granted us through the divine action in the event of Jesus

Christ, must not blind us to the wider working of God in the world. In any event, "the love of God is broader than the measure of man's mind." We can be no less generous than God whose care knows no bounds. Hence we must respect and honor any and every manifestation of God's loving concern in this world of ours, whatever or whoever may be the agent for its accomplishment.

Countless men and women, simply because (albeit unconsciously) they *are* God's children, often show "no little kindness." They often "kindle a fire" and "receive gladly" those who are in trouble, in need, suffer oppression, or feel lonely and neglected. They do this often enough with no thought of reward but simply "because it is raining and because it is cold."

Let us not be too narrow in thinking about the ways in which God gives "grace and comfort," help and strengthening, to people in all places and at all times. We should thank God for them and for what they do. What is more, we should join with them in their readiness to show kindness, to stand up for justice, to work for goodness, to create beauty, and to seek truth. For in all these there is a working of the same God whom we have come to know, through no merit of our own, but because in the divine mercy God has made it possible for us to understand the nature and action of deity through Jesus Christ—in whom, as our next chapter will argue, there is a focal and decisive disclosure and release of the divine Love "for us men and for our wholeness."

III

Called by Your Name

We who are Christians are those who are called and thus identified by the "name of Jesus." Or if we are not that, we *want* to be called by that name—or sometimes even, we *want* to want to be called by it. I have put it in this way because (as we shall see shortly) the degree or intensity of our allegiance may vary from time to time; we are not always faithful in the fullest sense.

To talk about "name" in Jewish thought was to identify someone by the disclosure which that name had made. It was also to have a certain relationship with that someone—at worst, it meant to be able in some fashion to control that someone. If I knew your name, I was given a capacity to know *you* in the deepest way. But of course in respect to deity, things were bound to be different. Nobody could "control" God. Yet it was possible so to know the divine character or nature that an intimate relationship could be established, with the initiative on the side of the revealing one and the response on the side of the person to whom the revelation had come. Thus for you or for me to say that we are "called by God's name" or by the "name of Jesus Christ" is for us to say that we *belong* to God or to Jesus Christ. To be a Christian, then, is to say that we belong to God *through* Jesus Christ our Lord; that is, we affirm that the God to whom we would belong is the God who has been enacted in human existence in the complex yet unified event which we indicate when we say Jesus Christ.

So we must begin our discussion here with some account of the basic Christian proclamation about that historical event in Palestine two thousand years ago and also with an understanding of the "stream of influence" (or the consequences) which the event has had in succeeding centuries, through the living tradition which is the Christian fellowship we describe as "the Church."

The discernment of Christian faith first received expression in the New Testament documents. These are our earliest, which is to say the apostolic, witness to what happened then and there. They focus on a Man who shared fully in the circumstances of his time and place and in the exigencies or demands that such a timed-and-placed existence imposed upon him. This was a *real* manhood, not in a meaning implied by later theological discussion in which it was often said that in Jesus God "assumed manhood." By using that adjective in this connection, I mean that it was possible to say—and there were people who did say—that the humanity of Jesus was only a pretended one, "assumed" in our modern sense of the word. But the response of the apostolic witness in the New Testament really makes such a view impossible. Whatever else may be said about him, this Jesus was truly and genuinely human, physiologically and psychologically, just as you and I are human.

Christian faith, however, has discerned more than that. The name—the "name above every name"—is for that faith not only "the name of Jesus," Jesus as the Man that he was. It is also, and pre-eminently, the name of that One in whom (to use again the phrase I have used earlier in these meditations) *God was enacted*, both to reveal or disclose or manifest the divine nature as sheer Love-in-act and also to communicate or release or "let loose" that very same Love into human existence. It did this in a fashion which was so definitive that it has been seen as decisive. In traditional Christian thinking, therefore, the total reality of the event of Jesus Christ has been called "the Incarnation," while the result in giving humankind the capacity to live in love and so find a proper fulfillment of human possibility has been called "the Atonement." We may not be enamored of those precise words; indeed, in our own day, devout Christian thinkers have found them troublesome, and have sought other ways of affirming the distinctive place and significance of the originative Christian event. But the deep insight of the "social process" which is the living Christian tradition has not been mistaken—or at least those of us who are "called by his name" must affirm this reality. But after all, we are not supposed to believe in "the Incarnation" or "the Atonement;" rather, we believe in the One about whom such words have been used.

Something more needs to be said here, however. In western Christendom, in which most of us have been brought up, the tendency has been to regard what happened in Jesus Christ as primarily, if not entirely, "the remedy for sin"—a sort of "divine rescue-expedition," in the unhappy phrase once used by C. S. Lewis, in which God has been intruded into the creation in an anomalous fashion to set right what has gone wrong in our existence. In the Eastern Orthodox tradition, however, and also in one strain of the western Christian tradition, another approach has been taken. For those who have adopted this other approach, the event of Jesus Christ is linked more closely with the general creative activity of God in the whole world and with the conviction that humans are "made in the image of God."

In the western Church Duns Scotus was the most eminent spokesman for this position. "The Incarnation" is linked by him with "the Creation" and not only with the "Atonement." Indeed, we might put it by saying that what occurred by God's act in Jesus Christ, and the human response to it, is another and a signal instance of the divine creative agency in the world. Here there is no anomaly but rather what elsewhere I have ventured to call "the classical instance" of God's working in the world. Deity is always active, always dynamic, always creative, always receptive, always in relationship with the creation. There is thus a continuing process in which deity and creation, God and humankind, are in contact one with the other—by divine initiative, on the one hand, and by creaturely responsivity, on the other. So the signal and focal action of God in Jesus Christ is to be interpreted as the implicit end and goal of what is potentially or partially going on elsewhere, and supremely in the human realm. To put it bluntly, even if humankind had not "fallen into sin," God would yet have acted in this fashion, to manifest his abiding purpose and to bring it to its climactic expression in human existence.

Undoubtedly some will regard such a position as dangerous. They may even dismiss it as "Pelagian," which means that supposedly it builds far too much on what is potential in humankind. But this is to misunderstand the point. We are *not* saying that humans, naturally and by their own efforts, can come to any such realization (or making actual) of their truest possibility. What we *are* saying is that God is the inescapable *prius,* the "first mover," who creates humans with this potentiality—they are "made in God's image." God also so acts for and in and with humankind that the event to which we Christians point—the event of Jesus Christ in its complexity and its unity—is at last brought about. Divine initiative and creaturely human response are both at work; but as always God comes first, to create and instill and awaken and lure and establish in a focal moment in history what for us Christians is revelatory and releasing of the divine character as Love.

Now it may be asked why I have gone into this discussion of what may appear to be too remote from ordinary experience. Is this not all a matter of "theology," using that word as if what is theological is abstract and without relationship to the concrete business of Christian living? After all, we are trying in this book to see the practical and "experiential" reality of Christian faith. Why should we then complicate things by such discussion?

To this the answer is plain enough. A practical faith which is not thought through is likely to be superficial. Without some attempt at a coherent and consistent grasp of it, intellectually and rationally, we may very well fall into merely prejudicial ways. Our firmest convictions may become nothing more than our preferred "hunches" or our often all-too-human wishes. The sort of discussion in which we have been engaging is a help to us precisely because it gives a certain "vertebrate" structure to our believing. We humans are not supposed to be like jelly-fish lacking the vertebrate quality that provides some definite form or shape for what we believe and thus also provides an intelligible grounding for what we do in worship and in prayer as well as in our daily living—out of what we "profess with our lips." Of course it is not in theology that we should put our trust. To do that would be to turn a living reality into a morphological description. It would be as if we substituted for a living thing like (say) a butterfly an account which would perhaps be scientifically accurate but would miss altogether the splendor of the thing itself—in the case of the butterfly, its color and its tremulous fluttering quality. Thought about these matters is not identical with living them out. Yet without such thought carried on to the best of our ability on the basis of our concrete experience, the result would be only a sentimentalized and thought-*less* way of being a Christian disciple. The two belong together: on the one hand, deep practical and experiential faith; on the other hand, a readiness to think through and to think out, so far as we are able to do this with our finite capacities, what is believed at the heart of faith.

So it is that when in the Compline office we dare to say that we are "called by [God's] name" defined in Jesus Christ, we are at the same time declaring that this calling is not irrelevant to the rest of our human experience, neither is it unrelated to what is going on in the world at large. Ours is not a faith in reason but it should always be a reasonable faith.

The requirement here is that we shall love "the Lord our God with all our heart and mind and soul and strength"—which tells us that there is no excuse for us if we simply refuse to use our minds as best we can, granted always that we shall never arrive at *the* truth in its essence. But then whoever thought that such arrival was possible for us men and women? To think that it is possible would be to become guilty of pretentious pride and arrogant claims to an admission into the secret counsels of God. We are to do the best we can, always ready to admit error and to acknowledge how partial is our understanding.

Precisely here is the point in the increasing concern these days for genuine Christian renewal. This is not a matter of trying to force ourselves to think in a fashion which is not possible in our differing circumstances. That is why I have ventured in what has gone before to suggest possible new ways of getting at the *real* meaning for us in our own time of the Christian's "being called" to respond to God's pressures, intimations, lures and solicitations. An old hymn found in many hymnals speaks of "new occasions" which "teach new duties." It might equally well be said that new circumstances, new perspectives, new awareness, not to speak of new knowledge, make this a *necessity* for us. Even the simplest Christian is included in that necessity, although his or her way of meeting it will not be technically informed or expertly developed.

If in Jesus there is a disclosure of the divine reality, in some fashion which is both decisive for us and definitive of how things go in the world; if at the same time there is a release, a "letting loose" into the world of human affairs, of the same divine reality; if, in a word, God is active Love—then for many of us a problem is raised, sometimes with dreadful pain. How can God be Love when there is so much that is wrong in the creation? How can God be Love when there is not only human wrong but also evil? No mere fancy of mistaken human minds but as a genuine *fact?* Something must be said about that. For we can affirm God to be Love, not by denying all this evil but *in spite of it,* recognizing it for what it is but still daring to claim that "the love of God in Christ Jesus our Lord," by whose name we would be called, is still the supreme reality and in the end will be triumphant over anything and everything that seems to contradict it. The next few pages will be concerned with this inescapable issue.

The horror of evil in the world was brought home to me a number of years ago when I was in Italy immediately after the earthquakes which caused terrible destruction and brought appalling misery to thousands of harmless men and women, especially in the mountain regions near Naples. It received a new emphasis in my thinking when I heard the report of a mother, living near New York City, who had suffered the loss of three children, one after another, in traffic accidents in front of her little house on a main highway. The mother had cried out, according to a newspaper account, "Why does God do this to me?" Her anguished words gave vivid statement to the problem with which we are concerned: God is Love, yet there are these terrible evils in the world which is God's. How? Why? we ask.

Implied in that mother's query, as in most of our questioning along these lines, is a particular picture of God and of the divine activity in the world, a picture which is deep in the minds of a great many people. In effect this picture respresents God as in complete control of whatever takes place. Hence God is omnipotent in the fullest possible sense; and the problem is simply to attempt to reconcile sheer power with utter love. If God is thus all-power, how *can* God be Love? And if God is truly Love, why does God permit such evils to occur?

One of our difficulties, then, is that we inherit a long history of Christian thinking in which God's omnipotence has been taken to mean that God either directly wills or permissively allows any and every happening to take place. That includes such things as earthquakes and traffic accidents. Hence God must be seen as responsible for all these. They take place exactly as they occur *because* God wills them to take place. In reaction from such a stark and terrifying picture of God, many people have become atheists who deny God altogether, while others so limit God's working that they regard deity as soft, easy-going, and undemanding, concerned only with giving immediate happiness to men and women. Both these positions seem to me false to the real Christian picture of the God whose name is declared in Jesus Christ.

Another difficulty comes from our reading the Bible without recognizing that it is the story of a gradual but genuine development on the part of the Jewish people in their conception of God and God's ways. If each and every part of the Bible, especially in the Old Testament, is taken as a direct and literal disclosure of God, the problem which is here being considered becomes intolerable. What we need to do is read the scriptural material in the fashion which Martin Luther urged: to see its validity in the degree to which it points towards God in Jesus Christ. Then the sections which portray God as sheer and almost immoral power loose in the world will come to be interpreted as the initial stage in a long and varied growth in the human understanding of God's nature and God's activity. From very primitive portrayals we move towards later prophetic affirmations of God as always acting justly in dealing with men and women; and finally we arrive at the conviction that God's fundamental character is *chesed* or "faithful loving-mercy." Otherwise—reading the Bible as "all of a piece"—we cannot escape our dilemma.

For an informed Christian faith God is no cosmic manipulator, no all-powerful tyrant, no inexorable controller of everything in the creation. It is indeed true that God is "the strength of creation" and the chief creative agency; but this is different from seeing God as willing evil, either directly or permissively. Rather, it is the certainty that God respects and honours the freedom of the creation, and that God is working in and through that freedom. At the human level, and also at every other level, there is a freedom which results in choices or decisions, some good and some bad; and these have their inevitable consequences, again, some good and some bad. I claim that this is the only kind of world that God *could* create, unless we fall into logical absurdity and therefore think of God as a cosmic tyrant and not a "loving heavenly Father" of the creation.

If now we return to the anguished mother, we need to ask how and why she allowed her children to run into a road where heavy traffic passed by. Why was there no fence or wall to restrain them? There is no need to introduce the divine will, as if that will *forced* her to neglect these or *forced* her children to run into the road in front of the house. Human freedom is real, both for the mother and for her children. Or if we think of the Italian earthquake, we can see that on this planet, even at the level of the natural order, there is a relative freedom—of course not a conscious freedom, like that of the mother and her children, but none the less a genuine freedom—which brings about happenings that are not inevitably for the benefit of the planet's inhabitants. This is the only kind of world that God could create, if there is to be real freedom in a creation that has its own integrity.

What is at stake here is our doctrine of God. The popular picture if often both unchristian and absurd. For a Christian who knows that "the name of God is Love" such as is disclosed and released in the event of Jesus Christ, God is not a tyrant; neither is God a sentimental "granddaddy." God creates a world in which there is a genuine opportunity for good to emerge; yet for God to do that it is also necessary that evil *can* emerge. For us humans, God is neither a dictator who sets out to make things difficult and horrifying, nor benign and spineless kindness. In Christian faith, when it has been realistic about things, God has been seen as here in the world, sharing in its anguish as in its joys. God is engaged in creating a world in which by necessity there are risks. And at the human level, God wants men and women to assume responsibility, to learn to choose aright, and to live in such a way that the good is augmented on every occasion.

What *is*, at any given moment, is not always "right." Here the poet Alexander Pope was entirely in error when he said, "Whatever is, is right" and that "partial evil [is] universal good." This is not true; it is unchristian as well. Often what *is* is very wrong. God's unfailing concern is to work to bring good out of wrong, to make love prevail where evil has been present, and to bring us men and women to act for these purposes. God is neither a hateful despot nor a reluctant agent; God is the caring creative agency in the world, as God is also the loving parent of those who live in that world. And God calls us to join with the divine working towards greater good here and now. Or in the words of St. Paul, "In every respect God works together for good with those who love him." Not only so, but God *always* works for greater good, even for those who do not love him or acknowledge or even understand what is going on. But about that we spoke in the last chapter.

We may now return to the point made at the beginning of this chapter. A Christian is one who wants to be "called by God's name" known through Jesus Christ. Or he or she is one who wants to want thus to be called. The degree and intensity of this desire will vary enormously from time to time and from person to person. How could it be otherwise, if God does not coerce us but rather invites us to respond to that supreme disclosure of the divine nature and name?

A great deal will depend here upon our particular physiological-psychological make-up. Years ago an old teacher of mine was accustomed to say that it was a lot easier to believe firmly at ten o'clock in the morning that at six o'clock! Some of us find it hard to respond at almost any time. But what matters is not this at all; it is the intention or underlying wish which is present in us. So I repeat that "to want to want" is of the highest importance. Many men and women for one reason or another do not just now respond to God and the movement of God upon them. But the real question is, do they desire to respond? Or are they lazily indifferent? When such an enormous issue is finally posed to them, would they in their deepest moments wish to be "called by God's name?" Ultimately, where do they stand?

Just here there are aids provided in the Christian community. About them we will speak in the following chapter.

IV

Firm in Your Faith

If a Christian is to stand "firm in [his or her] faith," with the assistance of the "grace and comfort of the Holy Spirit," it would be foolish to reject or to neglect what the Prayer Book calls "the means of grace." These are the various ways in which God's love as active towards us, and the strengthening or refreshment which enables us to live as Christian disciples, are made available. Briefly, they are the sacramental acts of the Christian tradition, coupled with our own effort in prayer and devotion with the response from God that such effort receives.

We are thinking in this book of many different aspects in the Christian life, as these are phrased in one way or another in the Compline Office. This is no theoretical discussion, even if from time to time (as in the last chapter) it is necessary to introduce themes that are theological in nature. But it is essentially a practical matter, this business of Christian living. Like all practical matters, it needs to be *practiced;* and the corollary of this is ready acceptance and a glad use of the practices which in the Christian tradition have been found of enormous value. Hence in the present section our attention will be turned to the liturgical worship of the Church, principally expressed through the Eucharist (or Holy Communion, Lord's Supper, or Mass), the use of other sacramental rites, and with these also the "personal prayer" which gives a wider context in day-by-day living.

If these are refused, there is every likelihood that we shall *not* "stand firm in [our] faith" but shall discover that it is growing weaker as the years pass by. For the traditional ways are not accidental or incidental to the reality of faith. They are for its nourishing and strengthening, so that humans may become Christian people. Or in splendid words from the Anglican Ordinals, so that they may attain to "ripeness of age in Christ," and thus become the instrumental agents to witness to God defined in Christ, and be the channels through which the divine love released in him may be effectual in the world. Thus to be "fellow-workers with God" is our specific Christian vocation.

Before we look at this sacramental observance, it seems proper to say something about the wider liturgical life of the Christian Church. I refer here not to specific rites but to the whole setting in which the Christian tradition has seen its worship, prayer, and manner of life. This word "liturgy" is from the Greek and means "a public work." At once this tells us that the Christian fellowship, while it is indeed made up of many people, male and female, is also a community whose activities are meant to be "public"—visible expressions of the continuing faith and witness to the world. In the second place, through its long history the worship of the Church has come to be ordered or patterned, accompanied by words and actions, and surrounded by as much dignity (and beauty too, whether this be in stark simplicity or in more elaborate rites) as is possible. This patterning is not done merely to gratify our human desire for such "decent" ordering, although that is entirely proper. Its purpose is to bring to the worship of God everything that will contribute to the divine glory in word and act, in art and color and sound—and smell, too, for incense has come to be part of much Christian worship in the Catholic line of development.

Since humans are not souls who are imprisoned in bodies but are body-soul or soul-body organisms, all this is entirely appropriate. If men and women are to be "firmed in their faith," they need every possible aid; one of these aids is precisely ordered worship in its dignity and beauty, with its changing seasons and their successive feasts and fasts. The "means of grace," insofar as they are sacramental, will more especially be given such an embodiment. Historically this has been a slow but inevitable movement. It takes place even in groups like the Society of Friends, where there is no "ornamentation" but the beauty of sheer simplicity and the evocative quality of a bare building in which, as Baron von Hugel once remarked, the very absence of signs is itself a sign of the transcendent reality of the God who is worshipped there.

Some of us are very much attracted by the wealth of symbols, the beauty of worship, and all the aids to worship which have come to us from the past. By being so much part of our existence, they help each of us to become what Romano Guardini, the noted German writer on worship and liturgy, liked to think of as "liturgical people." The embodied nature of our worship speaks to our own embodied existence. We are enriched in our discipleship and, if we keep a right proportion in our observance, can become ever more firm in our faith through these outward things. Here our inner life is strengthened by "external religion," as George Tyrrell called it, which is part of the treasure inherited from long centuries of Christian practice.

On the other hand, some of us are more likely to find an expression of our deep faith through the exercise of our mental faculties and the use of our will. In our own day many are urgent in their wish to discover ways of speaking christianly which are more immediately in accordance with contemporary knowledge and thought. Those of this type of mind may be either conservatively minded or more radically-minded; one group wishes to hold on to inherited fashions while the other wishes to engage in the work of *aggiornamento* or "up-dating."

But there are also those, of whom the present writer is one, who would stress for themselves and would find enormous value in the liturgical actions of the Church, while at the same time they are much concerned for the task of "re-conception"—and this book represents just that sort of effort. The setting for such persons, of whom again the present writer is one, as they do what they can towards re-conception, is within the grand liturgical tradition, not against it or apart from it. Hence they are devoted to the age-long worship of the Church, with its dignity and color, its beauty and its appeal to the senses—so natural and right for embodied humans—while they seek in various ways to make that worship more suitable for people who live today. They are zealous in their intellectual efforts as they seek to see how the focal and decisive quality of the originative event of Jesus Christ can more suitably and satisfactorily be interpreted and presented in the period in which we live. All the way through, they know that without the Church's continuing worship, centrally in sacramental expression, they would lack a base for their re-conception. If Karl Barth was right in saying that all theology must be of the sort that can be "preached," they would wish to affirm that all Christian thinking which is worth anything must spring from and lead back to the perennial worship of Christian people, as through the various "means of grace" they both adore God in Christ and also are strengthened in the firmness of their commitment in faith to him.

Having said all this, we may now turn to some of those observances which are of such assistance to Christians. I shall not discuss *all* the sacraments of the historic tradition, since that would entail far too lengthy an account but also since those for whom these words are intended will themselves probably have been both baptized and confirmed and by having received such baptism and confirmation will have been grounded in the "social process" which is the Church. Into that community they have been admitted; in it they stand; and through it they receive the strength and power to live as Christians. Neither is it to the point here to comment on marriage and ordination, appropriate for such persons as feel themselves called to this or that "estate" of life. Hence we shall confine our attention to three of the traditional seven sacraments: the Eucharist; confession and absolution which each of us needs (nowadays this is more suitably known as "the sacrament of reconciliation"); and anointing or "unction" for those who are ill and for those who are approaching their death. Each of these is a means within the Church's established existence for "firming us" in the faith in God's name known to us through the event of Jesus Christ.

In the Eucharist we have to do with *another* event, for it is best interpreted as an "action" in which things are done, rather than a rite involving an entirely mental exercise, with the point of helping us to *think* of Jesus Christ as One who lived in Palestine centuries ago and whom we reverence as the One in whom God is disclosed effectively for our wholeness. We *do something* in the Eucharist; and that doing is the way in which the presentness of the *historic* event is given in a *contemporary* event. We have already seen that ours is an "eventful" world, in the literal sense of that world. It is not a static, fixed "thing" creation. We can more confidently say this today because, quite apart from the way we do in fact experience the world and ourselves in the world, scientific labor over many decades has been largely a demonstration of activity, happenings, occasions, or occurrences as basic to how that world goes. Thus it is no accident either that the sacramental rite in which we know him most intimately is also an event. Action and event go together; indeed they may be taken as different ways of saying the same thing.

As an event, then, the Eucharist (like all events) is marked by what can be styled a memorial quality. It is a consequence of what has taken place in the past and it brings that past into the immediacy of our present; although on each occasion there is also a splendid novelty which makes it fresh and vital. Thus the Eucharist is a "memorial" (*anamnesis* is the usual word employed in theological discussion, and its meaning is precisely "memorial") of the originative event of Jesus Christ in its full integrity. This tells us that the action is not focused solely on the passion and death of Jesus; on the contrary, as they used to say in the Middle Ages, "the *whole* life of Christ" is the "sacrifice of the Cross." Everything that took place during that life was preparation for and foreshadowing of his total self-giving in Calvary. So it can be rightly said that in the eucharistic celebration the whole Christ is remembered and brought into our contemporary experience.

That total self-giving of Christ is communicated to those who assist at and are recipients of the sacrament. There is communion here between God active in Jesus Christ and us humans who receive; there is also communion amongst all who are caught up into what God accomplished through the originative event. The result is that those who are "called by [his] name" are sent out, "to live and work to God's glory."

In this sacramental observance we are given the spiritual strengthening which enables us to remain firm in the faith of Christ. In our own strength we should not be able thus to stand; we are far too feeble, far too self-centered; far too confused and troubled by what in the next chapter we shall call "the changes and chances" of our mortal life. But we are not left alone, to struggle on by ourselves. This "means of grace," by which the faithful loving-mercy of God released in Jesus Christ is given, provides "the food for wayfaring men"—as the New Testament idiom implies and as one of the popular eucharistic hymns phrases it—of which we stand in need if we are to continue loyally as Christian disciples.

Here is the reason that attendance at the Eucharist is so important. Catholic Christianity has made it a matter of obligation to be present at least weekly at that sacrament. Increasingly, we must gratefully acknowledge, members of the more Evangelical or "reformed" denominations are being brought also to see this point. As in Catholic circles there is a realization that each main celebration of the Eucharist should include a homily or exposition of the Christian gospel, so also in those other circles there is a renewed understanding that the Eucharist is central as the specifically Christian act of worship. Both Martin Luther and John Calvin, in their own day, intended that this should be the case. To fail in that regularity of attendance, with the receiving of the consecrated elements of bread and wine as part of the action, is to imperil our Christian profession. So once again the Eucharist is given for our strengthening in the faith.

It is natural that this should be so. For a sacrament is "an outward and visible sign" of a spiritual and non-material reality. That is how humans exist: the lover embraces and kisses his or her beloved and thus both expresses the love between them and deepens and vitalizes that love. Goodness is known to us only through good people acting rightly; truth only through statements which humans make; beauty only through objects which convey beauty to those who behold them. It is entirely natural for God to employ natural means to convey a reality that is more than material. So it was also with God's activity in Jesus Christ where a natural and human existence became the channel through which God decisively moved towards us. In traditional language, this is known as "the sacramental principle." It applies to all those sacred signs, indeed to the entire worship of Christians (and for others too, in their own particular religious allegiance and life), quite as much as to the Eucharist and behind that sacrament to the meaning of the life of Jesus himself.

Secondly, there is "the sacrament of reconciliation." Of course God forgives apart from the use of that "means of grace." God's "nature and property," says the old collect, "is always to have mercy and to forgive"—and God forgives before ever we turn in repentance to the divine compassion. In fact the reason for repentance, in the deepest sense, is our knowing that we are *already* forgiven, "while we were yet sinners," as St. Paul tells us. This forgiveness brings us to sorrow for what has been done to impede the divine action in the world and what breaks the free and open relationships which God intends between us and that action. To see that one is thus forgiven makes the sinner feel shame for his or her wrong-doings, wrong-thinkings, and wrong-speakings. When I was young the devout priest who regularly heard my confession told me that I should never forget how much such wrongs had "wounded the heart of Jesus." To realize that wounding, he said, would bring me quickly to repentance and the determination for an "amendment of life." The language he used may have been somewhat sentimental; but I have found the meaning which that language brought vividly to my young mind very compelling in the course of a long life.

It is good for us to have a specific channel in which we may confess what after examination of our lives we see to have been wrong with us; and it is good to hear from the designated agent of the Christian community, an ordained minister or priest, words which bring home to us and thereby make real for us the divine forgiveness. This does not imply that the priest himself forgives and absolves. Rather, the priest is the agent of the Christian fellowship in pronouncing on God's behalf the reality of reconciliation with God and our human sisters and brothers. Few things can more strengthen and refresh our discipleship, making us "firm in faith," than that assurance.

Then thirdly, there is unction or anointing. When anybody is ill, it can be difficult to keep the lamp of faith burning bright. When anybody is approaching death, this can be even more difficult. Of course this is not always true; there are some men and women for whom bodily sickness can bring a deepening of conviction, not least if through the years that deepening has already started. Certainly there are not a few who as they come towards death are enabled to renew their faith and face the future with remarkable equanimity. For most of us, however, there is need of some "means of grace" which will be for our strengthening. And just here the possibility of anointing, with accompanying prayer, may prove an invaluable resource. In such anointing there is the renewed assurance of divine acceptance and hence a renewed possibility for commitment to the God who so graciously accepts frail, sinful, inept humans.

The Church, in its Catholic line of descent, has always stressed this, although until recently "unction" was generally reserved for persons who were actually dying. Nowadays, on the other hand, its use has been extended so that anyone who wishes to benefit from it may ask for it. Interestingly enough, with the revival of concern for the spiritual aspect of the healing process in human life—sometimes exaggerated, alas, so that ordinary medical or surgical means have been thought insignificant—the ancient practice of anointing, with its New Testament grounding in St. James's epistle, has been seen as part of the perennial wisdom of the Christian centuries.

These sacramental rites do not stand alone. For a number of men and women who are not ordained but none the less are part of the Church's universal priesthood—and that includes every member of the Christian fellowship—there is the delight they have taken in using the "Daily Offices," whether in the longer form which is more often found in "religious houses" or in the shorter Matins and Evensong which the Anglican Reformers (and some of their continental friends) devised out of these older compilations. There are parishes where such people "drop in" from time to time, while some of them make it a daily habit. Many of us can testify that few practices have been more effectual in strengthening our Christian allegiance; and for myself, the services held in the chapel of King's College in Cambridge have become so much a part of my existence that when I am unable to be present I feel a great deprivation. In the New Testament book called Hebrews, Christians of the writer's time were exhorted not to forsake "the assembling of [themselves] together." The regular daily prayers of the Church, known in ancient times as *Opus Dei*, "the work of God," are a "means of grace" which do much to make us "firm in our faith."

There is also personal prayer. I have not said "private prayer" because for a Christian, conscious as he or she must be of belonging to a fellowship, anything taken to be entirely private would be a contradiction of such belonging. But prayer *can* be personal, in that it is undertaken by each person for herself or himself, without others present during the time devoted to it. There is no need here to dwell on such personal prayer, since it is a part of the life of anyone who professes and calls himself or herself Christian. Each one will seek a way of praying personally that is both appropriate and helpful. And there are hundreds of books to help in this exercise.

Besides this, there is spiritual reading, not only of the Bible but of other literature. Such reading should be intelligent as well as attentive. Often the urge to read the Bible has been predicated on an almost literalistic understanding of Scripture, with the assumption that all parts of the Old and the New Testaments are direct messages from God and have an equal claim upon us. That is to forget the truth that the Bible is the dramatic story of a long development in human response to divine activity in the affairs of the world; it is also to forget what we have seen was Martin Luther's insistence that the Bible is to be read in such a way that material in any part of it is to be accepted as it points towards God's self-disclosure in Jesus Christ. Some passages are more primitive in teaching, with little to do with that self-disclosure: it is the great main themes or motifs which help most, since these indeed do point towards what happened in Jesus Christ and in consequence of his coming. One may hope that someday somebody may summon up the courage to produce an "abridged Bible" (although to some that may seem almost wicked to suggest), which will contain only those passages which plainly help towards a fuller grasp of the central Christian convictions, without bothering the reader with material that can hardly be reconciled with those convictions and which often speaks about God in a fashion that no earnest Christian would presume to accept. We need not blame the writers and compilers of the Scriptures for including such material; on the other hand, we need not foolishly seek to make it our own.

As to wider "spiritual reading," I may for a moment be personal. The books that speak to my condition are such as Mother Julian's *Revelations,* some of St. John of the Cross and St. Theresa, the splendid writings of the French Père Jean de Caussade, above all his *Abandonment to Divine Providence,* (an unfortunate translation of the original French title which means not "abandonment" in our modern sense but an offering of self to God in our own given time and place and circumstances), and in more recent times the books of George Tyrrell, Baron von Hugel, John Baillie, and the like. Reading such books, slowly and attentively, is a way of "firming us" in the faith. In their own way, they are "a means of grace."

I return now to the point made as we began this chapter. It is absurd to assume that anybody can become "firm in [his or her] faith" if that person makes no attempt to use whatever means are available for exactly that purpose. Thomas Henry Huxley is reported to have said cynically that "it doesn't take much of a man to be a Christian." Presumably he meant that there are no requirements for integrity or honesty, such as he would have found in scientific inquiry. But in a remarkable way what he said was a tribute. *Any* person, rich or poor, wise or simple, of any class or rank or culture, can be a Christian. Thank God for that. Huxley's added comment is also to be noted: "But it *does* take all of him." Yes, it does indeed. One way in which that requirement is seen is in the necessity to use to the fullest extent every available "means of grace," for the strengthening and refreshing of our human life in faith.

V

The Changes and Chances of This Life

Human existence for all of us is cluttered with many things. This existence of ours resembles a Victorian drawing-room, filled with knicknacks, souvenirs of visits to seaside resorts, photographs of family and friends, little tables with curios on them, spindly chairs in every corner, over-stuffed armchairs from which it is hard to get to our feet, and so much else which makes it appear outlandishly over-crowded. Our existence intellectually is cluttered with ideas, bits of information, pieces of irrelevant knowledge, and vast numbers of factual or theoretical data. Our spirit is crowded with anxieties, fussings, worries, hopes, aspirations, insecurities, and uncertainties. In every part of our existence we resemble some depository for accumulated possessions. We lack any focal point of existence. What we need, if our existence is to be brought into a significant unity and human integrity is to be achieved, is exactly what Kierkegaard said was the basic meaning of purity of heart: to learn to will one thing.

Coupled with this personal "clutteration" is the confusion and disorder of life in this mortal world. It is changing constantly so that we have difficulty in discovering what if anything will abide. It is a world of chance, in which we are never certain of what is coming next and are obliged to live out our days without the security of a self that can face up to the exigencies of each succeeding moment. All of us are caught up in this situation; it is inescapable—not because we are sinful so much as because we live in a finite world where each event or occasion has its goals which often can bring about real conflict between or among them.

Surely each of us knows that something like this is the case, quite obviously with others and with ourselves too when once we have stopped our hectic activity and contemplated our existence as honestly and frankly as we are able to manage. So it is that in the Compline office we pray for a deliverance from this clutter, confusion, and chanciness. Otherwise we cannot find rest nor can we meet our final end with equanimity.

There is nothing evil or wrong about change as such. In a world which is dynamic and not static it is only to be expected; and indeed Cardinal Newman has a famous passage in which he says that "to live is to change; and to be perfect is to have changed often." Perhaps the last clause in that saying is somewhat exaggerated but it makes a point: perfection is not immobility or inertia but is to be found in growth and development—*if* these are along the lines that promote fulfilment of potentiality and realization of good. What is confusing about change for most of us is that we do not have any such sense of right growth or development; we arc "anxious about the morrow" simply because it is unpredictable. Neither is there anything intrinsically wrong about chance, if this means only that ours is a world characterized by risk and hence requiring courage in face of an uncertain future. The wrong comes in only when the risk is so extreme that we fear its consequences; it sometimes seems too much for us and we are uncertain and once again can become confused and anxious.

Much more important in our thinking about "changes and chances" as disturbing equanimity and poise is the fact of our human sinning. Sin is not a consequence of a changing and chance-ful world. Rather, it is a matter of our own attitudes and the actions which result from them if they are not the kind that genuinely promise us a way to true human existence. We shall now say something about such sinning.

When St. Paul in writing to the Romans asks how to be "delivered from the body of this death," he is speaking of the kind of death which we experience when we are denying our deepest human nature and are finding our contentment in that which ultimately will not, because it cannot, satisfy our true desires. His is not merely a cry of despair, although his words obviously speak of an inner conflict between human possibility and human achievement. None of us is without some experience of the conflict. We know that there are possibilities that are compelling, attractive, enhancing, and ennobling. We know that we ought to be, as we are called to be, full and complete men and women. At the same time we know equally well that we do not and indeed cannot achieve an existence like that. Great literature is filled with material which speaks of this conflict. T. S. Eliot's poetry has it for a main theme; W. H. Auden wrote frequently about it, lamenting that our human desires are "as crooked as corkscrews." The novels of Dostoevsky, to take but one other instance, largely center in the realization of this conflict. Our real problem as humans is not that we are stupid but that we are filled with cupidity; it is not that we lack clarity of mind but that we fail to live with true charity of heart. Our perspective may be right, much of the time; but our willing is enfeebled and we are frequently ready to settle for the easier path. We are inadequate; we are also in defection from our truest human self-realization. Or as Martin Luther phrased it, we are *incurvati in se*, "twisted in upon ourselves." Our basic problem is just there.

I have put this in what may seem a very secular fashion; and I have done this purposefully, since for many men and women the old talk about "sin" and "sinning" conveys little meaning. If it is to make sense to them, if it is to speak directly to the condition that is theirs, we can best approach it through just such secular language. Yet ultimately, what I have been saying is nothing other, nothing less, than a description of the dreadful reality of our human sin. Or to put it in more specifically religious idiom, when any one of us looks at himself or herself in the light of the sheer self-giving which is symbolized by the figure of Jesus Christ on the Cross, we know very well that we are far less than we might be; we are shamed by Christ's goodness in action and we recognize that we are failures. We have "done those things which we ought not to have done; we have left undone those things which we ought to have done"—and if we are honest about ourselves we know that *in us*, in our unaided and entirely human efforts, "there is no health." That may sound extreme. But which of us would dare to claim that he or she is "all right," without fault or flaw, without failure and defection from the best offered to us and available for us?

This business of human sin is behind our inability to face the "changes and chances" which are bound to be present to us. Hence there is discontent, often a sense of desperation. I make the claim that to know this experience is part of our being human. We are not contented animals; we are made so much "in the image of God" that we cannot rest content in our own condition of self-seeking and self-assertion.

In his *Confessions*, St. Augustine put this truth in a sentence which has become famous but which is usually incorrectly translated. What he says is this, "You have made us to move *towards you*, O God; and our heart is restless until it finds rest in you." I have underlined two words, "towards you," because that is the correct way to translate the saint's *ad te*, which in Latin always mean movement in the direction of whatever-it-is which follows the preposition *ad*. The familiar translation says "for you;" but in Latin that would be *tibi*, not *ad te*. The point is important because it shows us that St. Augustine was very much aware of the way in which human existence is a dynamic affair, always moving towards what is taken to be the fulfilment or satisfaction of deepest desire. The deepest desire of any of us is for "the good" which will make us truly ourselves in the most inclusive and enriching way. And what is that "good?" Surely in the ultimate sense it is God and God only, who is the "joy of man's desiring." To be with God will establish each of us firmly and really as genuinely human.

The age-long Christian conviction is that in our human condition of "in-curvature," about which Luther so rightly spoke, there has been an inbreaking on God's part. That is what can put things right for us and with us and in us. In our faith the inbreaking is known in the event of Jesus Christ, where God is disclosed and released in what we are sure is a decisive way. But it is not only there that the inbreaking occurs. As I urged in a preceding chapter, what happens in that event is the "classical instance," the signal occasion, the indicative moment. Through it we are brought to see what God is always up to in the creation, above all in the human existence which is our own. Because of this we can have renewed confidence and come to live our lives courageously because we can live them with a basic certainty.

Although the event of Jesus Christ does not stand alone, but is an opening to us of how God is always working in the world, that event is indeed of signal importance for us. What we need is a vivid and compelling disclosure and release of divine love-in-act. Without such a disclosure at a given time and place there might be the possibility that we are "kidding ourselves" by engaging in fanciful speculation or wish-fulfilment; and that sort of thing never "saved" anybody. The Christian point is that in the human existence of Jesus—in its totality including birth, teaching, doings, death, and rising-again—the transcendent and unsurpassable reality we call God has indeed acted. In the long-continued God-human relationship, this is a particular, and for Christian discipleship a special, moment. The victory which God purposes us to share over our self-seeking, self-willing, and self-assertion, here receives supreme manifestation. Our weak, despairing, confused, defective human striving is met here by divine response, just as the very presence of our human desire for genuine good is a sign that God has planted in us a yearning for that same unfailing good.

Because this is the case, the disciple of Christ is enabled to accept herself or himself and enabled also to accept others as equally God's beloved children. Why? Because in the first instance God has accepted *us*, "just as we are," without making any demand upon us beyond our believing that this is so. Theologically this is styled "the divine prevenience." God comes first, God takes the initiative, God invites and wants human response, God lures us towards what God wants us to seek and to find. Or better, *to be found of.* Our human responsivity, says Christian theology, is inspired and enabled by the Holy Spirit; it is that Spirit who gives us "grace and comfort" and makes possible for us our answer "Yes."

There are many different ways in which such a certainty—or better "certitude," since certainty suggests far too much a logical or intellectual proof of the matter—has been interpreted and stated in the history of the Christian Church. But these theories about what is called "atonement" or "redemption" are not anything like so important as the simple given-ness of our being "freed to love," as I prefer to phrase it. *That* is what gives a grounding for our human sense of life's value and significance; and that is what brings us to the place where "true joys are to be found," despite the insecurities, uncertainties, ambiguities, and defections by which human life is so greatly plagued.

In the next chapter, we shall look more directly at how it is that "God's eternal changelessness" fits into this picture. That phrase from the Compline office can be greatly misunderstood, as we shall see; it requires careful examination in the light of the main Christian assumptions about God, the world, and ourselves, if we are to get it right. At the moment, however, it will be worth our while to say more about human existence in a world which is characterized by "changes and chances."

Here a useful beginning may be made by thinking of a familiar prayer in Anglican Prayer Books. That prayer was originally prescribed for use on the Sixth Sunday after Trinity, although in recent revisions its position has been altered so that in different parts of the Anglican Communion it is ordered for other Sundays. Here it is, in the old Prayer Book wording by Thomas Cranmer: "O God, who hast prepared for them that love thee such good things as pass man's understanding: Pour into our hearts such love toward thee, that we, loving thee above all things, may obtain thy promises, which exceed all that we can desire." Cranmer omitted one phrase from the ancient Latin collect which he was here translating. In the original Latin it runs *amantes te in omnibus et supra omnia*: "loving thee in all things and above all things." Why Cranmer failed to translate the full Latin text is not clear. What *is* clear is that in leaving out the words "in all things" he seriously disturbed the fine balance of the Latin. By that omission he implied (whether consciously or unconsciously) that genuine Christian response to God in love entails a rejection of the natural world and of human affairs. Insofar as that implication has been followed, a *false* otherworldliness has been introduced into the picture. The unceasing activity of God in the created order, along with the equally unceasing activity of God in all human life, has been minimized or neglected or (at worst) denied. This has led, or it can lead, to a separation between the redeeming of humankind in Jesus Christ and all the rest of God's revealing and saving work in the world at large. That there is a distinction here is not to be denied; that there is a separation here is a fatal misunderstanding. Let us turn, therefore, to consider the divine creativity in all its variety, so that we may put the event of Jesus Christ in the proper context.

In his interesting and attractive book *A World to Gain* (Darton Longman and Todd, 1983) Dr. Brian Horne bravely argued that "the union of God and man in Christ is to be seen not as something added to the material universe, introduced, as it were, to correct a plan that had gone tragically wrong; to the contrary, this union is the culmination of the creative work of the Father" (p. 18). In this connection he quoted a passage from the great Bishop B. F. Westcott's *The Gospel of Creation*, published as long ago as 1886: "It can be fairly maintained that we are led by Holy Scripture to regard the *circumstances* of the Incarnation as separable from the *idea* of Incarnation and to hold that the circumstances of the Incarnation were due to sin, while the idea of the Incarnation was due to the primal and absolute purpose of love foreshadowed in the creation." In such a purpose "sin was contingent." Or, to put it in words which do not require the use of the traditional incarnational language, that Christ-event is a decisive indication of God's abiding purpose to work in and through creation, both to disclose the divine nature and to effect a release of the divine love in the world and in human affairs.

It follows, as Dr. Horne pointed out on the same page of his book, "that grace is not a kind of repair work performed on a damaged machine, not a kind of spiritual tonic to provide individuals with the necessary energy for living their dying lives," but rather that grace "flows from [the] self-communication of God to man in such a way that man actually shares the life of his creator;" and that *this* is the purpose for which man was made. Dr. Horne was saying, in a different idiom from that which we have used, that creation and "Incarnation" belong together, rather than that there is (as so often has been taught in western Christendom) such a connection only or at least primarily between "Incarnation" and "Atonement." Of course it is through what God has done in Christ—"the work and benefits of Christ" as we have known them—that we come to reckon with who he is. He *is* what he *does*, we may rightly say about God. Yet what God *does* is more than "redeem humankind;" he is the creative source, the continuing support, and the final end for the *whole* world.

Dr. Horne rested much of his case on the insight of the ancient Greek Fathers of the Church and on what is still affirmed today within the Eastern Orthodox tradition. So have we also done at many places in this book. For the Eastern branch of Christendom seems to have taken a more balanced view of things than we in the west. And by citing the unhappy Cranmerian omission of words from the Latin collect I have done two things: I have indicated that in the west there was also originally although not always obviously a similar insight to that of the Eastern Church; and I have indicated that by putting excessive emphasis on God's supposed "apartness" from creation, Reformation thought has produced an imbalance which has been unfortunate not only for our theological understanding but also for the spirituality which is inevitably associated with that theology.

In spirituality or our way of devotion and discipleship we humans have great need to be given the strength and grace to face the "changes and chances" experienced in "this mortal life" with honesty and with courage. They need not be the total threat that often they are taken to be. They may very well be seen as marks of a finite creation, inevitable if and because God lets that creation respond in freedom to the divine invitations and lures. When it comes to our human sinning, the horror and tragedy of our defection is undeniable. At the same time we may be encouraged to see that even in this tragic side of human experience there is a continuing presence of God, grounding us in the divine activity and seeking constantly to assist us in overcoming the wrongs to which we are so plainly prone. What is more, Mother Julian once again had a word here which speaks to our condition. She ventured to say that "sin is behovely," by which she was not for a moment commending it or implying that God is indifferent to it. She was urging, with all the vehemence of emphasis so frequently found in her writing, that God can use such sinning "for his greater glory." *If* we sin, *because* we sin, *since* we sin—and do this against our best interests—God is by no means helpless. On the contrary, God's infinite love for the creation and for us in that creation is such that God has ways of using what has been done amiss, to the end that a greater and more wonderful triumph of love may be achieved. In that sense, it is not mistaken to speak (as does an old Latin prayer) of the tragic "fall of man" (to use conventional words) and the resultant sinning of humankind as *felix culpa* (the happy wrong) which secured for us, thanks to God's unfailing loving care, "such a great redemption." One might almost say that precisely in our realizing how great may be our human falling, we learn how high is our human destiny as God purposes it to be.

Dr. Horne put all this in the words which he quotes from the ancient collect appointed in the 1928 Book of Common Prayer in England: "Almighty God, who didst wonderfully create man in thine own image, and dost yet more wonderfully redeem him: Grant we beseech thee, that as thy Son our Lord Jesus Christ was made in the likeness of men, so we may be made partakers of thy divine nature . . ." This collect seems to sum up, in the idiom that has become traditional in western Christianity, the double truth of which I have here spoken. The spirituality of the Christian ought to be based on the realization that in the very "changes and chances" which each of us knows so well and in the sad human situation of defection from the divine purpose for our lives, we are yet promised what another collect calls "the fruition of thy glorious Godhead"—which is simply to say, remembering the ancient and primary meaning of "fruition," full "enjoyment." The Westminster Catechism was right when to the question, "What is the chief end of man?" it responded, "To glorify God and enjoy him for ever."

The view which associates creation with God's action in Jesus Christ is known (as I noted earlier) as "Scotism," since it was advocated by the medieval theologian and philosopher Duns Scotus in the thirteenth century. The other view, associating the event of Jesus Christ primarily with redemption, is called "Thomism," because St. Thomas Aquinas defended it in the same century. But these terms are not quite accurate, although they have been used for centuries. As a matter of fact, Scotus was vividly aware of sinfulness in humankind; his concern was only to establish the right priority. In my judgement he was correct in what he urged. On the other hand, St. Thomas Aquinas, while saying emphatically that the "Incarnation was ordained as a remedy for sin," could also say (in the very same article in the *Summa Theologica*) that because "the power [of God] is not limited God could have become incarnate even if sin never existed." His reason for taking the other position was simply that he believed that the Bible pointed unmistakably towards it. Here he may have been in error and Bishop Westcott in the right in thinking that in Scripture sin is regarded as "contingent."

But these are probably somewhat academic matters. I wish to make some comments on another point, however, which has much to do with Christian spirituality as well as Christian thought. Once again we may use Aquinas as a starting-point. The Angelic Doctor is discussing whether or not the created world, always with God as its creative source, has or has not always existed. He can see no theological-philosophical ground for rejecting the view that it has always existed. But, again turning to his reading of the Bible, he is brought to reject this view since he believes that the Bible plainly teaches creation at a given moment of beginning.

Is this an important issue? To my mind it is. How *do* we read the Bible? That is the prior question. If Aquinas could have seen the Genesis material about creation, not as an historically accurate report of something that happened in the past but as a pictorial (or a mythological) way of affirming, in the idiom natural to the writers of that ancient biblical work, that *from* the primal Love that is God all things ultimately come and upon it they all depend, he might have taken a different position on the question he was discussing. So also when in a later chapter we consider the so-called "the last things," we shall see that the Revelation of St. John the Divine is equally a pictorial and mythological way of declaring that *to* God as cosmic Love all things move and into God they are received and accepted and used. In both instances this more intelligible way of interpreting Scripture helps our Christian spirituality, because it delivers us from incredible historical talk and frees us to understand more profoundly what creativity and receptivity, both in and of God, are all about. At first it all may seem highly theoretical; but in the end it turns out to be enormously significant in the life of Christian believing for men and women of our own day.

VI

Your Eternal Changelessness

The splendid words of one of the collects for the Compline office asks that we humans who are "wearied by the changes and chances" of our lives in this world may "find rest" or "repose" on "God's eternal changelessness." Those words have often, perhaps usually, been interpreted as if they referred to deity as monolithic, inert, static, sometimes even as unconcerned about the immediacies of affairs in the creation. But their profound significance is quite different; and in this chapter we shall explore that meaning, particularly as it indicates what it is about God that gives to our existence a genuine stability.

Sometimes I have thought that it is unfortunate that the noun "changelessness" is used in that collect. How much better it would be if we spoke about God's utter dependability, God's unfailing character as goodness and love, and the divine ability to triumph over whatever would deny or damage or destroy those things. But the word is found in the prayer, and it is used so much (and indeed liked) by worshippers who gather for Compline that we must see what we can make of it.

First of all, it does not mean that God is a "metaphysical rock" (if there can be such a thing!) who has nothing to do with life's "changes and chances." On the contrary, for Christian faith God is very much a sharer in the vicissitudes of human and earthly experience. If the divine enactment in the humanity of Jesus Christ tells us anything, that is central to the story. Far from being remote and unconcerned with these troublesome human lives of ours, God is involved in them, so that it can even be said that there is nothing which can happen to us, whether for good or for ill, which God does not know "from the inside"—not as an external observer but as a genuine participant.

Neither does it mean, in the second place, that the divine existence lacks vitality, energy, and the "processive" quality which characterizes *all* existence, from the tiniest "puff" (as Whitehead said) up to deity itself. "To be" is "to become," in every range and at every level, creaturely and divine. Far from being inert or static, deity is very much *alive*. And when God is called "perfect" this word tells us, not that God is above and beyond all change but rather that God can and does experience the effects of change yet without being less than fully and truly a self. God's divine perfection does not lie in a self-contained and self-sufficient existence; it lies in the divine ability to deal with whatever happens in the most adequate manner, so that the divine purpose is not distorted nor diverted from moving towards its own supreme objective. That objective, we have already insisted, is nothing other than "amorization" or the bringing of love to the creation in as many ways and in as many places and for as many creatures as are included in that creation.

In the third place, God's respect for the freedom of the creation and equally the freedom of those of us who exist in it tells us that the divine reality not only knows what change is all about and experiences its results, but also faces the "chances"—and the risks and uncertainties—which necessarily attach to the exercise of just such freedom. God can indeed "over-rule" the world; yet this is done by persuasive means, through lure and attraction and invitation and not by the use of coercive force which would compel the creatures, against their will, to do what is intended for them in order to promote their own best good.

The biblical portrayal of God, developed through long centuries of Jewish history, shows God to be anything but inert, inactive, non-participant, and entirely self-contained and self-subsistent. God *cares;* God *loves;* God *labours* continuously with and for and in the created order. The tragedy in much historical Christian thinking has been in its too-ready adoption of other ideas, mostly derived from some (but not all) aspects of hellenistic thought. The marriage of such ideas with biblical insight has been a disastrous one whose result has turned the scriptural emphasis on "the living God" into a concept of God which is an intolerable and non-scriptural idol. Even in the use of the biblical material an unimaginative reading of many of the texts has contributed to this idolatry, by changing the portrayal of God as unswervingly righteous and wanting the creatures to reflect that righteousness into a deity whose nature is that of a "moral tyrant," making demands which often seem to bear little if any relation to the concrete facts of human existence, punishing in a horrible way those who presume to disobey these demands and providing rewards which themselves are not very pleasant. For "heaven" with such a God would in itself be "hell" for creatures to whom freedom has been given, for whom respect has been shown, and who are always the children of the divine love.

What then can it mean to speak of God's "eternal changelessness?" I suggest that our answer here is to be found in seeing that God is entirely and always faithful in love, acting under every circumstance in accordance with that love. The only meaning that can be given "changelessness" in this context—and it is an entirely valid meaning—is that the divine love never changes in its character. It is *always* and *unfailingly* love-in-action. Yet, in its being precisely that, the divine love must of necessity adapt itself to particular conditions. In that sense it is changeless *in its nature* but changing *in its relationship* to the world and its inhabitants.

A truly perfect human life cannot resemble Aristotle's "great soul" in the *Nichomachean Ethics* who constantly gives but never is open to the action of the beloved towards him. Such benevolence is a horrible thing. Far from being "great-souled" such a human person would be intolerable. An old teacher of mine used to say that while it is indeed "more blessed to give than to receive," the whole tenor of the stories about Jesus is to show that it is "most blessed to share"—to give *and* take, to be in fellowship with others or with another. If this is true in human relationships, we may dare to claim as Christian believers that it is true *a fortiori* of God, the creative source, the constant companion, and the ultimate destiny of the creation. Thus there is "changelessness" in *one* sense; there is continual "changefulness" in *another*. And all the way through, the reality of God remains exactly what it is: namely *chesed* or (in the words of the Authorized Version of the Bible) "faithful loving-mercy." *That* remains constant and unvariable; upon it we may indeed "repose" and in it we may indeed "find rest," whatever happens by way of "changes" in mortal life and by way of "chances" in our human existence.

I have said above that the word "dependable," or an insistence on "divine dependability," is the fundamental affirmation which is conveyed religiously speaking through the inherited term "changelessness" as applied to deity. We may now break this down into several significant stresses. First there is the divine indefatigability—the unresting, continuing, ceaseless activity of God in carrying out his purpose of "love-making" in the creation. For us to be caught up into this working of God, finding in God's will "our peace" (as Dante put it), is the way in which men and women are given what might be phrased (with due caution, to be sure) "cosmic security." By this I do not intend security in the sense of deliverance from all problems and difficulties and complete removal from the experience of earthly "changes and chances." The point is that human existence can depend upon God's working which never "lets one down," no matter how hard that existence may be. Nor is this to be taken as an excuse for failure to do all in our human power to ameliorate the conditions for life. God is not to be "used" as if there were some sort of divine substitute for human effort.

Second, we may speak of the divine indefeasibility. Here I am talking about God's possessing sufficient resources to meet and to handle any and every creaturely situation. When things are at their worst, they are not entirely hopeless. Why? Because within the divine life there are strengths and capacities which can and will be employed always to bring the best out of what happens. This may not be obvious to us in every instance. Much of the divine working in the creation is not readily open to our human inspection. Yet the Christian tradition, building here upon Jewish conviction and its fulfillment in the originative event of Jesus Christ, is prepared to claim that "God *is* working his purpose out"—and we should underline the "is," precisely because of our confidence in the unfailing reality of divine power which is always love-in-act concerned to strive for true goodness, real justice, rightness of life, and all that makes for the fulfillment of creaturely possibility.

It is hardly necessary to say that to rest upon such dependability— the indefatigable and indefeasible nature of the divine working—is to be delivered *from* "faithless fears and worldly anxieties," as the prayer in the American Prayer Book phrases it, and delivered *into* "the freedom of the children of God." It is also to be made courageous to face whatever happens, precisely because "underneath are the everlasting arms." Thus a Christian need never be afraid as he or she seeks to do what seems required in any given circumstance.

But it is important to emphasize once more that this is not at all to say that our problems can be automatically solved without effort on our part. Nor is it to say that we shall have no serious difficulties with which to reckon and no demanding issues whose resolution hangs upon our own human decisions. God does not work against these, in the sense that he supplants them by an imposed, divinely-given response to the problems, difficulties, issues, and the like, which are simply part of the situation which men and women necessarily must deal with.

Confidence in God, trust in the divine purpose, dedication to the divine will—maybe with less than total giving of self, which in any event is often beyond our powers at this or that moment, but with as much of ourselves as we can honestly manage to give—is the way in which our lives can be properly strengthened, enriched, and ennobled. Here the contemporary Christian will find great encouragement if he or she looks at the great Christian saints of the past. These saints are "the many witnesses" who help us "to run the race that is set before us." Above all, for the Christian there will be an unfailing "looking unto Jesus, the pioneer and the completion of our faith." In that Jesus, central to the total event of Christ's enactment of the divine action in human experience, we see just such a dedication, commitment, and confidence. What is more, through him, again seen as central to the total originative event, there has been released into human existence "the strength and power of love," signally and decisively for us men and women, providing a more than merely human strength for "the living of these days," as Dr. Harry Emerson Fosdick phrased it in one of his hymns.

Changelessness, then, is dependability. Yes; and we might also say reliability and trustworthiness. To be able to rely on someone is to see in that person a consistency in character and in action which provides us with an opening for confidence. To call someone trustworthy is to say that it is possible always to "count on that person" in all circumstances and at all times. So it is that the old Latin "office hymn" (from St. Ambrose of Milan) rightly speaks of God as "the strength of all creation." God binds things together and gives them coherence. Or to sum it up, the ultimate "repose" for human life is in God who in all that he (or she) says and does, and in every range of created existence, can be recognized as "true to character."

I have written "that which" but it is much better to use personal pronouns here. For it is not *that which* but the *One who*—and here we can as well say "she" as "he," for in God there is the reality of those qualities which stereotypically we style "male" and "female," brought together in one inclusive self. God is dependable, reliable, trustworthy, in whom we find abiding rest and a deep inner peace amidst the turmoil and confusion of the world's affairs. The basic content of those qualities in deity has been stated earlier. It is love-in-action. To say that these qualities with their content as love-in-action are "eternal" is to indicate that the proper adverb to use about them is "always"—or "faithfully."

We need to reiterate that to live with this as the *leit-motif* running through every day of our existence is also to see that in and behind the "changes and chances of this mortal life" there is a basic drive or pressure which can handle these changes and face these chances without losing its own specific character. I have said that God adapts the divine purpose and acts within the world in such a fashion that conditions are met precisely as they are, without twisting them into something else. Here is honesty and clear-sightedness. God is not blind to such changes, neither is God unaware of the risks which the creation includes in its "creative advance" (to use a phrase of Whitehead's) into novelty.

Each of us knows very well that if there is to be such advance into novelty, there is bound to be an uncertainty about the future. We may think that we can grasp the main intent or "the big picture" but the details incident to the coming of that future are not determined in advance. This is to insist that ours is not a world where (to quote Ronald Knox's limerick) "everything moves in predestinate grooves." Of course God *knows;* and in one sense God knows *everything.* Yet that knowing is of things as they really are: the actual as actual and the potential as potential. Thus God cannot know what is going to happen as God knows what has and is happening. God knows only what is knowable and in the way in which it is knowable. The potential is now knowable save in its potentiality; only the actual is knowable in precise detail.

For the life of Christian discipleship, there is exactly that unpredictability which is the condition making the "chances" of existence so real, and even so troublesome and perplexing. But surely we ought not become too distrustful by that openness. Were it not present, human existence would be a dull, drab, repetitive affair; it would be boring or tedious. Perhaps there is a sense in which it would be good, as certainly it would be comfortable, to see everything "laid on the line." It would save us a great deal of worry if we were sure that tomorrow will be exactly like today. Unhappily, we cannot have that assurance. Life is not at all like that; and only a stupid or blind person would assume that it is.

This tells us that there is a freshness about human existence and hence a similar freshness in our Christian living. "New every morning is the love our wakening and uprising prove," wrote John Keble in a familiar hymn. The divine love is always new, appropriate to the new day; so also our response must be new and appropriate. This need not suggest that there are not sufficient regularities and con-sistencies in our day-by-day human existence; of course there are. But they are tinged with a certain surprise and newness. That makes the business of obedience to God an adventure into the partially unknown. And if it *is* an adventure, it is also fun. Some may be horrified to think a word like "fun" can be used about the business of being a Christian. Yet why should it not be used?

If the complications and complexities arising from "changes and chances" are too severe, then of course there is only confusion and damage to our integrity of purpose. So also when there is the wrong-doing which we call sin, there is a further probability of our feeling inadequate and certainly defective. Yet it may be salutary that we should come to understand this. After all, no human can be so pretentious and so silly as to think that he or she "has it all made." We can learn a great deal about humility when we recognize that there are such complexities and confusions and complications, as well as such inadequacy and defectiveness. The comfort here is that by depending upon God's reliability and trustworthiness, we can still go on facing each successive moment of our life without damaging fear.

Finally, the Christian confidence which we have stressed in earlier pages sees that in God, and in God only, is the final destiny of all things. In what the Compline office styles "the celestial brightness" in God as God, there is "the harmony of harmonies," so that what might have been devastating conflicts are made into significant contrasts with all the color and brilliance which such harmony with difference brings about. As the various colors in the spectrum are a breaking-down into particulars of an all-encompassing reality, so in human life there is a refraction of the brightness which is God. Conversely, in God there is the harmonizing of all those fragments in a glorious vision of beauty, so profound that we can only get hints of it here and now. "The many-colored splendor" of which Francis Thompson's poem speaks is in God; *our* eyes miss "the many-splendored thing." For us here and now this is a "dazzling darkness" (was it Traherne or Vaughan who said that?)—just enough brightness to cheer us and strengthen us; yet always for us a *mysterious* brightness apprehensible only by the eye of faith.

It is "by faith" that we humans walk the ways of the world, not "by sight." So St. Paul said; to this our common experience also testifies. If things are that way, why should we wish them otherwise, only deluding ourselves or claiming to know more than is given to mortals to know? This is not an easy lesson to learn because our stubborn human insistence on our own capacities gets in our way. Learn it we must, however; we must be ready to acknowledge that we are "lower than the angels" even if also we are the beloved children of God.

In such a faith, we can rest back upon God's "always-faithfulness," the divine dependability and reliability and trustworthiness, the divine resourcefulness for meeting whatever happens, with the assurance that "in the end"—which is to say, in God and not (as many would like to have it) "after a long time"—"all shall be well . . . and all manner of thing shall be well." Mother Julian was given in her *Revelation* or *Shewing* that supreme confidence. To some degree, yet never perfectly and completely during our life in the here-and-now, we can share that confidence, resting back upon "the eternal changelessness" which redeems all "the changes and chances of this mortal life." To this a sincere Christian disciple can only say, "Amen" and "Thanks be to God."

VII

Your Celestial Brightness

It is fascinating to observe how frequently the imagery of light is found in the Bible. In both Old and New Testament it appears again and again. God "creates light;" God is hidden "in light;" Christ is "the Light of the world;" God "dwells in light unapproachable;" we have been brought from "darkness into light;" in the heavenly city God is "the light" which supplants all other means of illumination. And it goes on and on, as any concordance will show and as Kittel's famous *Word Book* demonstrates. Nor is it only in Scripture that this imagery is used. In almost every language and almost all literature, light is taken as a basic image. So it is entirely natural for us to find such talk in the Compline office, where those who are "the children of light" are to eschew "the works of darkness" and to be conscious of God's "celestial brightness"—a light which is unparalleled and yet is intimated in all other experience.

We can see that one use of this imagery is to express the divine transcendence. God is intimately in relationship with the creation, as we have emphasized again and again. God is no remote and absent deity who only on occasion enters into and plays a part within that creation but is One who is *always* there although apprehended in varying ways and with differing sorts of intensity. Yet the reality of God is inexhaustible. We might put this by saying that when we become aware of God's active present-ness on any given occasion, we are aware at the same time that there is a "more" than that instance can manifest. From out of the unbounded divine life this or that activity takes place; but the divine life itself is not entirely contained in or operative through that instance. There are many created lights; all of them are reflections of or channels for *the* light which is heavenly and is nothing other than God. The God "who makes light to shine out of darkness has shined in our hearts;" and the Christian would say that in a distinctive fashion, so far as he or she can know, the event of Jesus Christ is above all the source from which we receive the "light of the glory of God." Yet there is always the "more," unexhausted and inexhaustible behind this human awareness of light.

Christian faith is utterly theocentric; it is directed towards and finds its center in deity and nowhere else. To some this statement may be surprising, because they have been accustomed to regard Christian faith as "christocentric," finding its focus in Jesus Christ and his work in the world. There is no doubt that Jesus Christ is central; but his centrality is precisely his accomplishment in bringing God near and making God real. Or better put, his centrality is in the divine reference of his human existence, where God acts with a speciality and decisiveness that has secured the response of Christian faith. Thus it would be right to say that as theocentric the Christian faith is directed not to God "pure" and without qualification of any sort, but rather to God defined by and given relevance in the originative event of Jesus Christ. Nevertheless it *is* theocentric.

Here it is worth noting that in the material we possess in the gospels which tell us about Jesus as he was remembered and reported in the primitive witness of the Christian community, he did not make claims *for himself*; the claim is always for God and for God's sovereign rule of kingdom. The Fourth Gospel doubtless has its source in a tradition or traditions different from those used in the first three gospels. In that Fourth Gospel claims *are* put into Jesus' mouth which might seem to make him speak of and for himself. But it is to be observed that even in the discourses which appear to suggest this, Jesus is represented as always dependent upon "my Father in heaven." He speaks and acts, not as if he were setting himself up in the highest place, but precisely on behalf of One "who has sent" him.

The imagery of light helps us here. If Jesus is called, as he is called in the Fourth Gospel, "the light of the world," it is because the light which he manifests and communicates is *God's* light, not his own humanly expressed light. So Jesus himself points, as it were, away from himself to God, God's will, God's purpose, God's sovereign rule.

Baron von Hugel used to warn against what he called "false Christocentrism." His acquaintance Paul Sabatier, the French Protestant sympathizer with Roman Catholic Modernism, spoke of the danger of "Jesuolatry." Both of them were alarmed to see that in so much Christian thought in their time, Jesus Christ was substituted for God and hence was all too likely to be made into an idol taking the place of God. Sabatier felt that the manhood of Jesus was enormously important but that what mattered above all was what God was doing in that manhood. Von Hugel, with his broad Catholic perspective, was concerned to bring the event of Jesus Christ into intimate relationship with the *whole* of the God-world and God-humankind movement. This is why von Hugel was generous towards non-Christian religious aspiration and belief. For him Jesus Christ in his impact upon history was "the implied goal and center" but not the exclusive or solitary instance of God-world and God-humankind action. Elsewhere there were many "God-given graces and mercies," as he phrased it.

To say this is to say something very positive about the other religious faiths of humankind; it is also to say something affirmative about what von Hugel was accustomed to describe as the "secular" ways in which God works in the world. These were not to be dismissed as irrelevant, whether it was a matter of Judaism, Islam, Buddhism, Hinduism, or any other humanly-practiced religious or secular modes of life. He would have rejected the "Christomonism" of Karl Barth's theology. Von Hugel's pupil Evelyn Underhill had something important to urge at this point. She insisted that if there were not some diffused or pervasive awareness of God generally at work in the world, it would be impossible to identify the event of Jesus Christ as a signal and specific instance of God's activity in the affairs of humankind. Whatever speciality was to be given to Jesus Christ must not be at the expense of this wide God-world and God-man contact. On the contrary, that wide contact provided the setting for whatever was to be affirmed in Christian faith about Jesus Christ.

An English writer of religious verse at the turn of the century, Mrs. Hamilton King, has these lines in one of her poems:

God may have other words for other worlds
But for *this* world the Word of God is Christ.

I believe that she was getting at something highly significant; but for myself I should have perferred to say that in and for other world-cultures than our own, quite as much as for "other worlds" (if there are such other inhabited worlds), God has "a word," even a "Word" (by which I mean a distinctive self-disclosure); but that for *our* culture and against our background, Jesus Christ can rightly be seen as a specific Word which addresses us directly and compellingly. By putting it in this fashion we shall be delivered from the "Christian imperialism" which Arnold Toynbee so vigorously denounced, as if we dared to claim that only to us who are in the Christian faith is it given to know God as God really is and as God really works. Nor does the adoption of this more generous and hospitable view for a moment deny the reality of what was done in the event of Jesus Christ. What it *does* do is to make us see that God is much more caring for all people and at all times than our narrow insularity would like to think.

Just before writing these lines I had a long conversation with a Japanese scholar who had come to Cambridge on a tour of the western world. This learned man belonged, he told me, to one of the prominent Japanese Buddhist sects, the one called after Nichiren, a Buddhist believer and thinker of the middle ages in that land. I asked him for some account of what this sect taught. He replied that it spoke of "the eternal Buddha" who he said was roughly equivalent to deity in our western sense. But because the eternal Buddha was inaccessible directly to humans, there had appeared a number of "bodhisatvas," which my acquaintance said could be taken to be "incarnations" of the eternal Buddha. One of these, whose name I did not catch, was the focus for members of the sect. Through that one, he went on to say, "salavation is given." When I asked him how this took place, he replied that it was by the grace of the Buddha as this awakened faith on the part of the believer. The consequence is eternal life, which he defined as the "negation of reliance on things of this world." (The meaning of Nirvana was just this, he said, and it is available for the believer.)

Now, I am not an expert in these matters; neither do I wish to say that there is a close parallel, even an identity, between such a religious faith and the "justification by grace through faith in Jesus Christ" about which Christian tradition speaks. Yet I am unable to dismiss the Nichiren sect's faith as simple error. Evidently it was already known in Japan before Christian missionaries arrived; it is a development of a type of Buddhism indigenous and natural for the Japanese mind. Surely the God and Father of our Lord Jesus Christ must have been at work there. In traditional language drawn from the ancient "fathers of the Church" in the early centuries of the Christian community, the *Logos* or Word of God was active in Japan, in a fashion appropriate to that place and those times.

I ventured to say to my Japanese acquaintance that I could accept what he had described as a genuine activity of the one and only divine reality, under whatever name and with whatever qualities that divine reality is known. As a Christian, I added, my urgent desire would be to assert that whatever was known of this divine reality in other religious faiths, the essential nature or character of that reality must be "of the same stuff" as what is declared, enacted, and released (as we Christians affirm) in the event of Jesus Christ. I was thinking here, of course, of the *homo-ousios* ("of one substance") of the Nicene Creed and giving it a wider application than is commonly done. The placing of *homo-ousios* in the Nicene Creed was a following of Athanasius' originally plain insistence that the divine Word "incarnate in Jesus Christ" was of identical character or nature with the same Word in God as the divine creative reality. Or in the language of light, the light which shines through non-Christian faiths and which is hinted at in various ways in the secular activity in the world, is not alien to but is the same light as the "Light of the world" which Christians discern in the originative event of their faith.

I have said enough on this subject. I must now proceed to speak of the way in which God's "celestial brightness" may be seen as the final destiny of the created order itself. As from that divine Light all illumination ultimately comes, so to that same divine Light all is ultimately directed. Light goes along with life and love in the Johannine picture, all of them differing ways of speaking about deity. The "eternal changelessness" which is the divine dependabilty, reliability and trustworthiness, the faithful loving-concern of God which is the innermost heart of deity, can also be styled "the celestial brightness" which gives its light to every thing creaturely—although never negating the freedom, responsibility, and dignity of the several channels through which the divine light shines.

What then can a Christian disciple affirm about his or her destiny, as well as the destiny of the entire creation in its widest range? This is the topic with which we now concern ourselves.

This is not the place for a detailed discussion of what in the Christian tradition have been called "the four last things"; death, judgement, hell, and heaven. Suffice it to say that (as we urged in the opening chapter of this book) there is indeed "an ending of the day" for everyone of us: we die and the book of our life in this mortal realm comes to an end. All talk about some supposedly "natural immortality of the soul" cannot negate that fact of death; and in any realistic portrayal of it, we must see that not only do we all die but that *all of us* (whatever it is that makes us human) dies too. There is more to be said, to be sure; but that more is not a denial of this total death. "Ressurection *from* the dead" is something else again; and we shall speak of this in a moment. And not only do we humans die, but we are judged or appraised for what we have been and done during our mortal existence. There is judgement or appraisal every day of our lives; there is the same when we come to the "ending of the day" at our death; there is also appraisal or judgement about what in the long run we and everything else have or have not contributed to the creative advance in the world. There is also what might be styled "the conclusion of the matter": the twin possibilities of complete frustration which is "hell" or complete realization of our possibilities which is "heaven." It is when we come to speak to these last two possibilities that the "celestial brightness" of deity becomes especially relevant.

I propose that in God's life there is a reception of that which in this world is accomplished. There is a positive reception or acceptance when that accomplishment is of the sort that can be taken by God and used by God because it is congruous with the over-arching divine nature as love-in-act. But there must be also a negative reception, which means a non-acceptance, into God of whatever has been contrary to that over-arching purpose. However, God is able—as human history demonstrates in its own way—to extract or distill from that evil a potential good. For a Christian the great symbol of this is to be seen in the way in which the evil of the murder of Jesus by hanging him on the Cross was turned into an occasion for good. This could happen because Jesus had dedicated his life to the point of being crucified in order that the divine will might be done. Thus the wickedness of humans can be turned to the goodness which God both receives and uses.

For Christian faith, the total event of Jesus Christ is not over and done with; it is not just a matter of past history which is now irrelevant and without significance. On the contrary, that total event, with its central point in the Man Jesus himself, has been "raised" into God. This is what resurrection tells us, when we succeed in "de-mythologizing" its details and the concepts in which it has commonly been stated. The total event of Jesus Christ is "in" God; it is incorporated into the very life of the deity, so that it makes a difference. In the first place, it makes a difference *for God*, because now God is able to use it in the furthering of the divine purpose in the world. God is not altered by this, as if he were somehow "improved" by receiving the event of Jesus Christ. What is changed is the way in which God may now carry on the relationship between deity and humanity. In the second place, things are different *in the world of human affairs*, because there has come into that world a "stream of influence" which is the Spirit of Jesus Christ released for and effectual within the world of history.

To be a Christian is to be participant in that ongoing stream, serving as a personalized instrument for its operation. In the concrete terms of human existence, what we are saying is that the Love which is God, the Love which in the originative event was enacted and expressed, is not finished and over. It has been "let loose" so that others are caught up into it and grasped by it; thus they can become its agents in this world's history, which all of us share. Or to return to the idiom of light, the "celestial brightness" which is divine is refracted in the created order at the human level in the specific fashion which was set forth and manifested in the event from which the Christian "social process" took its rise. What is more, that same light is in itself a judgement upon us: "Light has come into the world and men have preferred darkness to light, because their 'works' are evil."

The course of history in the centuries following those days in Palestine has been altered by this event. There has been the newly-concentrated and specific "power of love," available to men and women wherever they have heard the "old, old story." That power enables them to live more fully, richly, and purposively, seeking always to show in their daily existence the same strength and power of love, with its inevitable corollary in a search for justice and an indefatigable effort to deliver others from oppression and from servitude to the base and ugly and wrong. There has also been established a standard or pattern which appraises each of us, both personally and in our social belonging. Have we made ourselves and has our society made itself an agency for love-in-action, with concern for justice and freedom from wrong by the liberation of humans from servitude both to their own self-will and to the imposition of the self-will of other persons through political, social, economic, sexist, and similar selfish attitudes and acts and conditions?

I return, as this chapter ends, to the imagery of light. In the time-honoured custom of prayer for those who have died, a phrase has often been used: "Let light perpetual shine upon them." God *is* light, as God is love and life and truth and goodness and beauty. To be in God, with whatever that may involve, is to be "in the light," the divine light which shines upon God's children as they are taken into his/her existence. I have written "whatever that may involve" for a quite simple reason. We dare not claim to know much about what reception into God includes. Many believe that it includes a conscious awareness of what has taken place on the part of those thus received. This is often called "subjective immortality." Some prefer to think that such conscious awareness is not a necessary part of the picture. For them the very fact of being received by God is sufficient and they would be content to be made participant in the divine existence even if they do not "know" this subjectively; this is often called "objective immortality."

I do not wish here to judge between these two ways of envisaging the matter. Why? My answer is that there are dangers attached to either view. If we adopt the former, with its talk about "subjective" and conscious awareness, we may assume that somehow or other it is *we*, not God, who matter. So "life after death" can become an exercise in self-concern, rather than a giving of self to the God who receives us. If we adopt the latter, with its stress on "objective immortality," we may conclude that it is only what we have done and not we ourselves who are valued by God sufficiently to be received into the divine life. In that case, we may be led to think that our own selfhood is irrelevant to the divine Lover.

To my mind, the best attitude is to put the stress on the reception into God, in the confidence that God, in divine love and care for the sons and daughters of humankind, may be trusted to do the best that *can be done* in the sort of world with which God is related and for the sort of people whom God so dearly loves. In our best moments, I venture to think, we are prepared to leave such matters in the divine hands, knowing that God is always "doing for us better things than we can desire or hope for." In any event, if God *is* the center, so that our faith is genuinely theocentric (seeing God as defined in the Christian event as "pure unbounded Love"), we are glad to say that it is to *God's* glory that we look—and let us recall that "glory," in the biblical sense, has to do with *light* shining "more and more unto the perfect day." The transcendent God is nothing other than "celestial brightness." In God's light we mortals even now "see light," so that "our footsteps need not stumble" (as an old prayer says). And "at the ending of the day," we shall be glad to say with Robert Browning, "And *with God* be the rest."

VIII

Into Your Hands, O Lord

Most of the readers of this book will be familiar with the "Three Hours" service held in many churches on Good Friday. Although recently this "devotion" has somewhat declined in popularity, to be replaced by more traditionally-oriented liturgical worship, it yet remains for a considerable number of Christian people a valuable way in which they may center their attention on the Crucifixion of Jesus and in doing so may renew their commitment to him. The words of the title of this chapter, "Into your hands . . .," are one of the so-called "seven last words of Jesus on the Cross." They are also used in the Compline office.

The "Three Hours" service was instituted in Peru in 1687 by Jesuits who were stationed in Lima; they planned in this way to commemorate Jesus' passion and death. The occasion of the institution was a devastating earthquake in Lima. The service was brought to England by the early Anglo-Catholic priest A.H. Mackonochie, who after serving curacies at Wantage and at St. George's-in-the-East, London, became the vicar of St. Alban's, Holborn. Mackonochie introduced the "Three Hours" in 1860 or shortly thereafter. It soon became popular; and hence the service was held at St. Paul's Cathedral in the mid-seventies of the last century. Thereafter its use spread, until at one time practically every parish in England and many Anglican parishes and other non-Roman churches overseas made it central to the observance of Good Friday. Large congregations assembled in church from noon until three o'clock, to hear meditations on the "Last

Words" and to kneel silently for the tolling of the church-bell thirty-three times at three o'clock, the traditional hour of Jesus' death.

I have given this brief history because that service is now not so frequently held; yet it is an extra-liturgical act of worship that brings vividly before our eyes the fact about Jesus noted in the Fourth Gospel: "Having loved his own which were in the world, he loved them *unto the end,*" comments the Evangelist, summing up in a brief sentence what Christian faith has seen to be central in the career of that One who is the focus of the event by which, as Christians believe, God acted decisively to disclose the divine nature and to release into the world the divine power of love, for the making-whole of men and women through their being "freed to love" and hence to live in accordance with God's intention for them. It will be worth our while to say a few words about that terrible scene on Calvary before we turn to the main topic of this chapter, which is prayer in a specifically Christian sense.

In the usual story of Jesus' passion and death—which is a bringing into a single narrative of material drawn from each of the four gospels—Jesus is represented as doing several important things. He forgives those who are making him suffer; he accepts a penitent robber or insurrectionist; he commends his Mother to his disciple John and that disciple to his Mother; he experiences thirst both physical and emotional; he expresses despair at what seems to be a forsaking of him by the God whom he served; and he commends himself to that same God. At the very end he says, "It is accomplished"—not "over-and-done-with," but as the completion of his life's work. The one "last word" which has troubled many is the saying, "My God, my God, why have you forsaken me?" which seems to indicate a loss of faith in the face of intolerable anguish and God's apparent desertion of him. But that "word" is in truth the most encouraging of them all for those who have discerned in Jesus an action of God in human existence. It opens up to the believer the wonderful assurance that in any and every circumstance and situation God is a sharer with humankind: "if I go down into hell *God* is there also," as a Psalm phrases it. Thus Whitehead's simple description of God as "the fellow-sufferer who understands" is made a visible and vital reality.

For our purpose here, however, the words, "Into your hands I commend—or commit—my spirit," are especially significant because they give us the clue to what above I have called "prayer in a specifically Christian sense." All too often prayer has been interpreted in ways that bear no relationship to the fundamental Christian understanding of God, the world, and human life. It has been seen as an almost magical incantation; or regarded as an attempt to pressure deity into giving us what we think we need; or as an effort to force God to alter the course of events in the world; or as "pestering the deity with our petitions" (as Dean Inge bitingly styled it); or as a sort of "last resort" to be used when every human hope has been shown to be mistaken or false. In consequence, a great many devout Christian people have been put in the odd position of believing in God and wishing to be God's obedient children, yet finding the inherited practice of prayer either meaningless or ineffectual. This has created a situation in which one of the chief "means of grace" has been neglected if not rejected.

What then *is* prayer in a specifically Christian sense? I suggest that there are one or two clues which will help us. One of them is to be found in the story of Jesus in the Garden of Gethsemene, where in agony he prayed about the inevitable arrest, condemnation, suffering and death which awaited him. Having asked in that anguish that he might be "delivered from this hour," he went on to say—and here is the clue—"Nevertheless, not my will but yours be done, O Lord." Unhappily this has often been taken to mean a passive submission to an intolerable destiny. Yet a careful reading shows that the stress is to be put on the words "be done." Jesus is saying that whatever may happen, what he most wants is that the divine purpose be accomplished and that he may be the agent for its accomplishment: "Not my will, but yours *be done*." Hence a first clue to Christian prayer is to see that it is essentially the wish and desire to be a fellow-worker with God in the doing of divine will—which is a will for love, justice, and the right in the affairs of the world.

A second clue may be found in the definition of prayer by St. John Damascene, taken up and repeated by St. Thomas Aquinas: "the elevation of the human soul [or mind] to God." This means that prayer should be seen as a turning *from* concentration on the world and its concerns *to* God and the divine concerns. It is a lifting-up of the human personality—for more than St. John's and St. Thomas's "soul or mind" must be in the picture if humans are both body and mind, stuff and spirit—into the presence of God, in order to "be with God," so far as humans can have that possibility. Thus prayer is a "being with God."

A third clue, which is particularly important for us nowadays, may be discovered in a splendid phrase used by Dom Augustine Baker, the seventeenth century English Benedictine whose "Holy Wisdom" was set down in a book of that name which appeared a few years after his death in 1641. In that guide to spiritual life Dom Augustine Baker defines prayer as "the attentive presence of God." The phrase needs some explanation. God is always and inescapably present in the world; as the primal source, the continuing of all good in creation. God is active everywhere and always. But we humans are necessarily much immersed in the affairs of the world, living as we do in a finite situation where we must act humanly with attention to the problems which are ours and must try to discover ways of handling these problems with some measure of success. For that reason, we simply cannot be aware all the time and on every occasion of the reality of God's active presentness with us. Hence it is essential that we set aside particular moments when we give "attention" to this divine presentness. Prayer is exactly that attention—hence it is our "attentive presence" to and for God, where God's unfailing presentness becomes clear to us. Thus prayer includes just such intentional concentration on the divine reality.

Even more crucial as a clue are the words which are attributed to Jesus on the Cross: "Into your hands I commend—or commit—my spirit." Jesus dedicated himself fully and completely to the doing of the divine will; but even more, he gave himself in equal fullness to God—and why? So that God might accept him in the divine love and give him a place in the divine life. In other words, Jesus is represented as surrendering both himself and his "work" (in its every aspect) into God's ever-loving hands. The point is that only in God can be found the true destiny of all human endeavour; and whether that endeavour is obviously successful or is a seeming failure it is *safe in God* who is affected by what goes on in the world and who can use it for the implementation of the divine purposes vis-a-vis that world.

If Christian prayer is interpreted along the lines suggested by these several clues, it will be seen as very different from much that is conventionally taken to be the meaning of our human praying. With that in mind, we can now say something about each of the commonly taught aspects of prayer: adoration, thanksgiving, confession, inter-cession and petition. We can also understand better—although in this chapter I shall not have space to discuss—what are often styled "the higher reaches of prayer," like contemplation of and even "union" with God, as found in the great mystics of the Christian tradition like St. John of the Cross, St. Theresa of Avila, St. Catherine of Siena, and many others.

The order in which I have listed these aspects is not necessarily the order in which each one of us will engage in his or her praying. The reason for this is that particular occasions will suggest that this or that aspect be made the starting-place. For example, if we are faced with some enormously difficult problem, it is quite likely that we shall begin with petition: if we are deeply worried about a friend or relation who is ill or in trouble, we shall probably start with intercession. Yet the order which I have given is surely logically the *right one* if we have recognized that for our faith God is the center and that our religion is therefore inescapably theocentric and not centered on ourselves and our human ideas, aims, wishes, problems, and difficulties.

Adoration, said Baron von Hugel, is what all genuine religion is about. This indeed is what *worship* means; the root-meaning of that word, from its Anglo-Saxon origin, is the ascribing of ultimate worth or value to something more-than-human, to God in the divine mystery and the divine self-disclosure. In that sense, adoration and worship are extroverting in nature. The French writer on the history of religious thought, Henri Bremond, has a fine phrase which is relevant here: "disinfection from self." To turn to God and to give God supreme value in our thinking and living is to be delivered from concentration on our self into a recognition of how things truly go in the creation. Nor is this an inhuman or unnatural exercise. If for instance I love another human being, I can focus my attention on that person and on that person's worth and I can find that my own life is somehow intended to be devoted to that other's welfare. I can forget myself for a short time by devoting my attention to the other—and far from finding this a disagreeable business I shall discover that my own existence is enhanced. This principle applies also to prayer.

Prayer as adoration is our so attending to the divine reality that we can say "Glory to God in the highest," seeing ourselves as always dependent upon that One whose "glory" is also seen in the whole of creation. Once we come to grasp this, we are led to thank God for "our creation, preservation, and all the blessings of this life." Our human existence is in itself a gift; so also is our continuing life in this world. But above all, as the prayer which I have been quoting goes on to say, we are thankful for "the means of grace," brought through "the redemption of the world by our Lord Jesus Christ" and leading us on to the "hope of glory." Not only in the daily experience which is ours but chiefly in the enactment of the divine Lover in the event of Jesus Christ, there is a self-communication of God to men and women— and indeed to the whole creation. Particular moments vividly indicate this self-giving; and for these we must be especially thankful. Thought about them and acceptance of them will then form a regular part of our praying. We are enabled to do what the *Te Deum* says is our privilege. "We give thanks to thee for thy great glory." To thank God that God is and that God acts is still another way of our being "disinfected of self," yet without in any way looking at ourselves as entirely useless or utterly hopeless. We are God's beloved creatures and children; how then could we dismiss ourselves, or any of our sisters and brethren, as of no importance at all?

I have just mentioned "the hope of glory" as one of the things for which we must be grateful. Here unfortunately there has been a considerable misunderstanding, as if that hope meant that we were concerned primarily with our own subjective and conscious future in what is commonly called "heaven." I have already said something about this; at the present we need only remark once again that our hope is *in God and in God's glory*, not in our own reward in some after-existence. As a friend of mine once commented, "It is the hardest thing in the world for us to come to recognize that God matters more than we do" and yet see also that this "mattering" is not at the expense of the human creatures but for their right fulfillment.

We come next to confession in prayer. That must be discussed with care, since some think it means a shameful groveling in God's presence.

Confession is really nothing but total honesty about ourselves. If we have looked at our human lives honestly, we are well-aware of our inadequacies and our deficiencies. It is not necessary to engage in what Baron von Hugel quaintly styled "spiritual flea-hunting" to know this. Once we have come to see something of the glory of God and the sheer goodness of God in action as disclosed and released in the event of Jesus Christ we know that we are pretty shoddy creatures.

72

We need not fly to the opposite extreme of saying that we are simply "a rotten mess," as some Calvinistic theologians have urged. To say that would be to deny that we humans are "made in God's image." The truth is that we are still made that way, but that we have soiled, and damaged the image. If we contemplate God's self-giving love exhibited in the One whom God has "elected as the Proper—or true— Man," the total reality of Jesus Christ but above all exhibited in the supreme act of self-giving of that Jesus on the Cross, we are shamed because we have fallen so far short of that human possibility.

Years ago, when I was confessor to a community of nuns, I used to suggest to them that if they looked at a Crucifix and said, "That's what God is; that's how God acts; that's what I ought to resemble," they would find plenty of material for honest confession. No tedious "spiritual flea-hunt" was required but simply acknowledgement that in the lives of each of them there was a self-centeredness, a self-concern, an over-weening pride and pretension, which was both shameful and hurtful. In our personal prayer we can examine ourselves in that fashion from time to time, to see how and where and when and why we have gone wrong. If we do that, we shall find renewed awareness of God's accepting and forgiving love. God cares for us in our very failures; God forgives us so that we may go forward towards the true destiny intended for us: which is "the measure of the stature of the fullness of Christ."

Prayer, then, includes adoration and thanksgiving and confession —not always in precisely that order, to be sure, but always deep in our praying. Then come the two remaining aspects of Christian praying: intercession and petition. The former has to do with others, the latter with ourselves. Here there is great danger to be avoided. We may assume, wrongly and very stupidly, that by our expressing in prayer what we think is needed for other people as well as for important causes and concerns and by what we think we ourselves need or want—by doing this we may assume that we can somehow "twist God's arm" to give us precisely those things. But God does not work that way. Even the beloved Son had to be "conformed" to his Father's purpose. So do we. Hence in our prayers for ourselves and for others, there must always be the proviso, "according to God's will."

In the collect for XIV Trinity in the old Prayer Book we pray for "the increase of faith, hope, and charity" in ourselves. That is what we ought to be desiring, above all else. This is how we humans are able to "obtain God's promises" which exceed all that we can easily know and see. Prayer is not a magic way of getting what we want; it is an urgent identification of self with God and the commitment of our existence to God so that the divine will may be done in us and also in the others for whom we pray, as well as in the great and compelling issues that we face in political, social, and public human existence.

Of course, since we are human and in our humanity are bound to see this or that need as urgent, we shall bring into our intercession and petition the immediacies which at this or that moment appear to us to be of high importance. Like small children, we do not really know what is best for us yet we must put into words or thoughts what we take to be that best. Sometimes, alas, our intercessions and petitions will be *very* childish. But they should always be *childlike*, expressing our dependence upon God. They can avoid being childish if we remember always "our ignorance in asking." I recall a good woman who regularly and devoutly interceded for others. That was good. What was wrong, though, was that in thus interceding she informed God exactly what this or that person should have done for them or given to them. Not only was this absurd; it was almost blasphemous. God, however, must be understanding of good intentions; so we may trust that God will use even such human silliness, by accepting such praying for what it is meant to be, for the better ends or goals that are both possible and desirable for those who do the praying and for those for whom prayer is offered.

How do intercession and petition work? The plain answer is that we do not know. Yet if we have become convinced that God is the great and urgent worker for good in the cosmos, we can think that in the divine economy there is room for requests. Furthermore, because God is the Love at work in Jesus Christ, that same God can be trusted to "accommodate" or "apply" the ways in which this working is done in the world. To repeat what was argued earlier in this book, God as sheer Love never changes in nature; yet God in bringing that love to bear on human and worldly matters can "adjust" it to the genuine needs of the creatures.

In the end, in intercession and petition as in everything else that is entailed in human effort, the main emphasis must be on what Père

Jean de Caussade used to call "abandonment to divine Providence."
To say that is only to phrase in a different idiom the title of this chapter:
to commit into God's hands ourselves, those for whom we care, and
the needs of the world, with the assurance that those hands are both
righteous and good. In a way, all praying comes down to that, even
when it is adoration and thanksgiving. It is the desire and readiness
to let God be and do, in us and for us and for everyone else quite
as much as in and for the creation at large, *the right thing*. Ultimately,
the point of our praying is so to attend to God as to see God as our
supreme good. The medieval saints and theologians used to say that
God is the *summum bonum*. Once we have come to grasp this
profoundly Christian—and indeed also Jewish—teaching, we can pray
freely and boldly, often mistakenly and always imperfectly yet with
confidence that in the long run and "at the ending of our day" God's
grace and comfort will be there. The "changes and chances of this
mortal life" are inescapable for us; but God is also inescapable, even
if not always rightly addressed and given the proper name. Thus we
pray in recognition of the divine "glory" which is in self-giving; and
by that very token, we pray for our own great good, the great good
of others, and the fulfillment of the divine purpose of amorization in
our confused and confusing human existence.

I have not stressed here (as I did in an earlier chapter) the value
that many of us find in the right ordering of our prayer in the traditional
daily offices of the Church. In Anglican circles these are Matins and
Evensong, in Lutheran circles similar morning and evening devotions,
and in the Roman Catholic Church the old "Breviary" offices. While
these are not designed for personal prayer, nor can they serve as a
substitute for periods of personal attention to God, they can be
enormously helpful in providing a pattern which, when followed
faithfully, gives a setting for all that we do in our attempt to enter
into relationship with God defined in Christ. If I may be personal about
this, I should say again that attendance at these offices in a college
chapel has meant more to me than almost any other experience of
prayerfulness. The lections from Old and New Testaments, the
recitation or singing of parts of the Psalter, the splendid canticles like
the *Te Deum* and the *Magnificat*, the beautifully worded collects
prescribed for the several seasons, feasts, fasts and commemorations,
somehow give a remarkable setting for whatever may be one's own

preferred ways of praying. Above all, by allowing the office as a whole to take place and sweep one up into the centuries of Christian devotion, one becomes more and more ready to offer to the God who is sheer Love the devotion of the whole heart and the willingness to be God's instruments in the world. I commend the use of these offices, either with others in a community or college or school, or simply used by oneself. To do this is to discover that one has been made part of a fellowship of devotion which supports and encourages one when one's own spiritual life is poor and inadequate. Surely this is part of the reality of the communion of Christian people which is the Christian Church, with every member in his or her vocation and ministry finding a part and place. Here is great personal enrichment; here also is a contribution to the continuing life of the Christian fellowship.

All our praying is an enrichment both of ourselves and of the Christian fellowship. For while we must pray personally, we must always pray as participant in that living tradition, that "social process" as I like to phrase it, in which each one has a part and place, in which each one "counts," and in which each one has his or her particular talent or capacity to offer for the fulfillment of the Church's mission in the world.

IX

Be Sober, Be Watchful

In the old texts of the Compline office in English—and of course behind them in the Latin original from which the English office is translated—the words are: "Be sober, be vigilant; because your adversary the devil goeth about seeking whom he may devour. Whom resist, steadfast in the faith." We have already spoken about being "steadfast" or "firm" in the faith. In this chapter we shall consider the sobriety (or earnest single-minded devotion) and the vigilance (or watchfulness) which should characterize the Christian disciple. But what about those words about "the devil?"

There was a time when most people believed that the world was populated by demonic forces or evil spirits—Luther's hymn *Ein Feste Berg* speaks of "this world with devils filled." There were *good* spirits too, of course; but many people lived in constant fear of the way in which demonic powers could and often did interfere in human affairs in order to damage God's sons and daughters. Hence one of their constant petitions was for deliverance from just such attacks. In more recent times "the devil" and his minions have been "de-mythologized" (as the saying goes) by and for most of us. That is, we do not deny that there are evil influences in the world of our experience but we usually think of them in a less vividly personal fashion, talking perhaps of inherited faults or wrongs, environmental pressures, and the like. Usually we are not thinking that there is a personal devil who seeks our destruction or hurt. We are indeed to resist these evils but most of us do not think that there is an actual *devil* whom we must resist.

Unquestionably the Bible talks in terms of demons or devils and of what is wrong in the world as often caused by "demon-possession." Jesus in his human mind must have shared in the patterns of thought common in his time. Hence he too spoke of "demon-possession;" and he seems to have regarded his healings as a "casting out" of such evil spirits. In Jewish understanding those spirits came between God and humankind; they must be expelled if men and women were to live happy, healthy, and good lives. Nowadays it is more likely that we shall see all such talk as non-literal in meaning. At the same time, thoughtful people will not dismiss it altogether, as if it had no significance at all. Rather, they will feel that, like so many biblical symbols and idioms, it is to be taken very seriously for what it testifies about common human experience, although not literally as if it were pictorially exact.

I have spent so much time on this subject because I wish in this chapter to emphasize the requirement that every Christian—and evey other human as well—needs to be alert, watchful, soberly aware of that which goes against his or her best good and by that fact also goes against the will and purpose of God for humankind. Only a foolish or blind person would say that such an attitude is mistaken; only a very optimistic human would think that there is nothing wrong in the world which a little more knowledge cannot take care of and eradicate. The day when an honest and thoughtful person could adopt such a rosy view is long since past; two world wars, disturbances in every part of the world with violence and outrage, depression and its social consequences, and much else in our experience have ended the period that has been called "halcyon liberalism." We are much more realistic about the presence of evil in the human world.

We are also aware of the presence of evil in ourselves. Thanks to advances in psychological knowledge nobody today would wish to say that there is nothing wrong about himself or herself. Most of us know very well that we are not all that we ought to be and could be. In fact that condition which older theologies described as "original sin"—a state of affairs in which human existence, into which we have been born and have our being, has a strong tendency to do "the wrong"—has been called the one Christian doctrine which can be empirically verified by every one of us.

There is, of course, a likelihood that people will believe that they themselves are pretty much in the right and will blame "the others" for what has gone wrong. One of our difficulties is that we seem to lack objectivity about *our own* ways and attitudes and actions; we like to assume that if only other people were as good as we are, with intentions as good as ours, all would be well with the world. In *Barchester Towers* Anthony Trollope observes how many who are "wise" in the ways of the world find a convenient excuse for their own failure in behavior and their own neglect to be watchful about their responsibility: "Wise people, when they are in the wrong, always put themselves right by finding fault with the people against whom they have sinned." Thus they can remain content in their stupidity and defection because they have already decided far in advance of any action of theirs that whatever they think or feel is certain to be entirely right and proper.

However this may be, the Christian imperative is that we should be alert to what is wrong in the world and aware of what is wrong in ourselves. We should be "sober" in our appraisal of the facts; and we shoud be "watchful" or "vigilant" so that we can avoid further wrong and seek to put ourselves on the side of that which makes for goodness, justice, understanding, sympathy, and love in the affairs of humankind.

The other side of this, however, is not to be forgotten. A Christian is or ought to be alert to and aware of those places and ways in which good is at work, sometimes almost invisibly. An old friend of mine used to remark that if we had eyes to see we should be able to find plenty of places and many occasions when such goodness was being sought or being done. The picture is not one of unrelieved gloom; there are still what St. Augustine called *vestigia dei*—"traces of God"—in the created order. Many of these are not *obviously* a fashion which both reveals the divine love and justice yet also veils these in such a manner that they *seem* to be merely human or natural. It is for the Christian, who has been grasped by the divine disclosure in the event of Jesus Christ, to give such "anonymous" working of God its proper name, not least in those instances where there is an overcoming of wrong by the power of good, where injustice is replaced by justice, where beauty emerges out of what has seemed ugly, where truth counters falsehood, where there is liberation from oppression, and where love overcomes what might have been only violence and coercion. In all this, a Christian's alertness will recognize an active presence of God in the world. And he or she will be vigilant in cooperating (St. Paul says, as a "fellow-worker") with that active presence.

Maurice Wiles in his *Faith and the Mystery of God* (SCM Press, 1982)—a book which is remarkable for its combination of deep Christian conviction, awareness of modern problems, and an understanding of the world in which that faith must face those problems— has these words which are relevant to our present concern about the disciple's vigilance in obedience to, or better in response made to, which is disclosed and released in the event of Jesus Christ: ". . . the parable of the cross points the human imagination to a vision of God as participant in the continuing conflict with evil, identifying himself at whatever cost with both the perpetrators and the victims of that evil. It is through the cross that he is most clearly seen as the God for whom nothing is expendable save himself" (p. 72). Thus to be alert to see God as engaged with the creatures in "the continuing conflict with evil," self-identified with those who are struggling against it, and (as Wiles says) ready to be "expendable of self" in this enterprise, is a necessary part of our total Christian allegiance. Somebody has written that the way in which we can come to discern this is by "keeping our eyes open and using our head." By that he meant that we need to open our eyes to those indications of the right and the good; and then as Christians to identify them with the more specific action of God in the originative Christian event. They will be interpreted as "of one substance with," "of the same reality as," that which in Jesus Christ God has "determined, dared, and done" in and with and for the creatures who are loved and cared for by a reality greater than the human or natural.

There is a human tendency, from which Christian people are not exempt, to take too much for granted. It is entirely possible for us to accept or acquiesce in what occurs, assuming that somehow or other it is "meant" for the best. That attitude, to be sure, is much better than to overlook such occasions; and it is a part of Jesus' teaching that we are often in the presence of God's concern for the world but without explicitly acknowledging it to be such. Yet Christian discipleship surely entails a discernment of the presence as *God's* presence in action. One of the results of genuine Christian prayer or devotion is exactly that discernment.

In another piece of writing I have spoken of the way in which a Christian has been granted what I there styled "a perspective," "a purpose," and "a power," whose result can produce the sort of life that has value and significance. Of course any and every human senses that his or her existence has a real value; this is part of what it means to be a conscious man or woman. Furthermore, every man or woman is so "grounded" in the divine reality that such a sense of value is given validity. But the Christian should be one who has been able to identify that fact, to become aware of its divine background, and willingly to engage himself or herself with it both for personal enhancement of life and for wider sharing with other persons. This kind of identification with its corollary in cooperative activity can make all the difference. "Whom ignorantly ye worship, him declare we unto you," St. Paul is said to have told the Athenians who heard him on Areopagus. The reality which is seen in all that is good in the world and to which all people of good-will have sought to respond, each in his or her own way, is the same reality declared in Christian faith to be "the God and Father of our Lord Jesus Christ." To be given the ability to *"name"* that reality in this way is to receive a new understanding or "perspective" on the world and on human experience. It delivers us from what may all too often be a "worm's eye" view of things. It also provides what I have called a purpose and a power. The purpose which is here known is precisely the aim and intention to cooperate with that cosmic good, so far as is humanly possible. And the power is nothing other than the power of love which now has grasped the faithful believer and enables that believer to express in act what in inner experience is at work: the self-giving and concern which strengthens him or her to face difficulties which otherwise might seem utterly insurmountable.

When we put it like that, we need not think that the task is made simple and easy. Of course not, since ours is a world which is inescapably difficult to work in and to work for. Nor will all our problems vanish away. In fact, things may seem more problematic, just as the task may seem more complicated and hard. If we have come to see the heights to which we humans may rise, at the same time we have come to see how appalling are the depths to which we humans may fall. Further, with a new perspective we shall be brought to the uncomfortable realization that the human dilemma is much more serious than it might have seemed if we had only that "worm's eye" view; while the awareness of the divine purpose of love can shame us into an honest acknowledgement of our own deficiency and a grasp of the enormously difficult job which awaits us once we have been able to identify the true purpose of the universe in and under God. And we know that in and of ourselves we are hardly able to remain open to the impelling action of the power which is available for our strengthening. So often and in so many ways even the best of us are all too ready to assume that "we are able of ourselves to help ourselves."

In this book we have been talking about Christian spirituality in its broadest sense. We have stressed the necessity, in such spirituality, of dependence upon God. Prayer is one of the ways in which we acknowledge that dependence and seek to be opened to the activity of God which will use us, despite our inadequacy and defection, for great and good ends. Attention to God, which is basic to all Christian praying, is very much at the heart of all this. Upon what or upon whom do we focus our thinking and feeling and doing? Much of the time, alas, our focus is not upon God but upon ourselves; and even when it is upon God we are all too likely to picture God after some model which is attractive to us but which may be devastatingly false. Our faithful praying can provide a remedy here; but it can do so only if we make central in our spirituality the picture of God as the sheer Love that "will not let us go" and that will not let us rest content with less than the best. That "best" is the reflection in our human existence of the sheer Love that is God.

If somebody has as model for God a tyrannical power, the probability is that such a one will acquiesce in the use of coercion in the affairs of the world. If the model is a moral dictator, there is a probability that such a one will be "moralistic," usually identifying moral requirements with what he or she thinks appropriate. If the model is aggressively masculine, what is likely to happen is that the one who adopts it will be aggressive and dictatorial and will also be unable to see that the feminine is as much found in God as is the masculine. In this last instance there is another probable consequence. Not only will there be a failure to grasp that God is gracious and accepting; there will also be a refusal to accord to women a place in the affairs of the Church. Most of the opposition to the ordination of women to the ministry or priesthood is based upon a fear of the feminine (often a notable characteristic of the *male* clergyman) and above all upon an exclusively masculine, patriarchal, picture to the deity. So we might go on. There is a close correlation between pictures of God and human ways of thinking and feeling and behaving. Equally, there is a correlation between pictures of God and the way in which the Christian Church is defined or described.

The dictator picture of God is associated with the notion that the Church is to be the ruler of society, so that its dictates will be enforced on all and sundry. This attitude is called in Roman Catholic circles "triumphalism" and has been ruled out by what was agreed at the Second Vatican Council. When the picture of God is moralistic, the Christian fellowship is likely to be understood as the proclaimer and defender of a narrow "moralism," with a hardened view of sinful humanity and a demand that everybody should "obey the rules," whether or not these have much bearing upon the concrete facts of contemporary life. When the picture of God is aggressively masculine, the Church is unable to recognize the role of women in its own life, being content to relegate them to a "helping" part but without granting them a genuine place in its ongoing tradition.

Sometimes the picture of God has been what might be styled "nostalgic." In that case, God is enamored of the *status quo*, so that deity is identified with the "backwoodsman" mentality. God prefers things to remain as they have always been! Yet Isaiah tells us that God is the One who says, "Behold, I do a *new* thing." The "new thing" may not be very attractive to those who wish to rest in "the old ways." Hence they will protest and complain whenever there is some proposal for novelty in worship or re-conception in thought or less rigid patterns of behavior. This negative position is not simply a matter of a liking for old and "tried" ways in life of the Church. It is also a fear that any change will be for the worst and that the Church will become only a carbon-copy of modern ideas and attitudes. But basically, the position is a rejection of the picture of God as the creative source of novelty in the world, along with the notion that somehow the only way to preserve genuine continuity is by an exercise in repetition of what has gone before.

We Christians are meant to be alert—that is, to read "the signs of the times." We are meant to be vigilant, not only in what used to be known as "definite Church-teaching," but also to the ways in which "new occasions teach new duties." As to "definite Church-testing," that all too often means, for those who mouth the phrase again and again, what somebody years ago wrote or said about Christian faith. With the clergy it is frequently simply a matter of remembering what they were taught in theological college, especially if that teaching had been given with an absolute assurance that it was *the* Christian way. As a matter of fact, however, anybody who is familiar with the long history of the Christian community knows very well that there has been great change over the centuries. Certain affirmations have been constant, to be sure: the reality of God; God's activity in the world of nature, history, and human experience; the decisiveness of the event of Jesus Christ in all its importance for Christian faith; the gracious forgiveness of God granted to sinful men and women; and of course other affirmations as well. Yet the ways in which all these have been interpreted and presented have varied a great deal. One of the remarkable characteristics of the Christian fellowship has been its firm grasp on essentials coupled with readiness—sometimes a rather reluctant readiness—to see that new times require new ways of understanding those essentials.

St. Vincent of Lerins is famous for the "Vincentian canon," which in Latin reads *non nova sed nove*, with an insistence on that which has been held *ubique, semper, et ab omnibus*. "Not new things but in a new way," said St. Vincent, with the conviction that "what has been believed everywhere, at all times, and by all Christian people" *is* the truth to which we are committed. As to the first phrase, we need to see that to say things "in a new way" often means that we must also say things which are genuinely "new" and not merely a repetition in a different idiom of what has been said in previous periods. As to the longer statement about "what has everywhere, always, and by everybody" been accepted, we need to recognize that this is not so much a question of definition or theological formulation as it is a continuing and constant experience of new life in Jesus Christ, shared with our fellow-Christians, and accepted as a consequence of what was accomplished by God in human existence in that Man of Nazareth. Life comes before all definition; Christian life precedes all theological formulation.

The faithful Christian will be "sober" in evaluation of the old *and* the new. The faithful Christian will also be "watchful," vigilant and alert to those places and persons where God is most wonderfully saying and doing "new things." These are not discontinuous with the things that God has already done or with what God will do in the future, but yet are also truly novel, requiring of all of us, whether we are simple Christians or professional theologians, liturgists, or moralists, that we open ourselves to the continuing but sometimes very surprising ways in which the one God moves towards and in the world and in human experience.

X

Your People May Glorify Your Name

I have no doubt that some readers will have found this book a little confusing. They will say that it is a strange combination of a treatment of Christian spirituality which shows deep respect for the inherited ways of devotion. But (they will say) it seems often to turn into a theological treatise, although they may be kind enough to think that it is not "up in the air" in doing so. In respect to this theological interest, too, they may say that we have somehow shown great concern for the historical tradition of Christian thought but at the same time have ventured to suggest new phrasing, even new conceptions, with a bold rejection of some of the teaching which has been generally accepted through many centuries. "What sort of book *is* this?" they may ask.

On responding to such a question and admitting the accuracy of the comment about the "strange combination" of practical spirituality, liturgical insistence, classical theology, and the enterprise of "re-conception," we may say something like this. Spirituality and theology are much more intimately related than many people have thought. It is simply not true that the life in discipleship is so simple that it raises no questions; neither is it true that thinking about the basis of Christian faith and its articulation in a coherent and consistent pattern is irrelevant to the following of Jesus Christ. *How* we understand these ultimate issues determines very largely how we pray. *How* we pray has much to tell us about what we can properly believe. An unthinking faith can lead to thoughtless devotion, while a lack of spiritual discernment can produce a kind of Christian thinking that has very little to do with the main emphases in the tradition to which we belong. Finally, without an attempt at what Pope John XXIII called *aggiornamento* or "up-dating" of our Christian convictions, done bravely but humbly, we may only demonstrate that we are not prepared to serve God with our minds quite as much as with our hearts and souls. Therefore I cannot apologize for the sort of approach taken in this book. I can only hope that my intention to be helpful in every way has been apparent to the reader.

In an interesting book by an American feminist theologian, Sallie McFague, published a few years ago, some suggestions are made that can help us greatly in this task of "up-dating." The author points out that the language of religion is primarily metaphorical or parabolic. By this she means that it takes something which we know in our human experience and then dares to apply it to our picture of God, knowing full well that *all* our human ways of doing this are bound to be inadequate and partial. The safeguard, she says, is that we should have *many* metaphors, *many* parables, rather than just one. Thus we are delivered from idolatrously identifying God with this or that particular idea which happens to appeal to us. But first of all, she says, Jesus is our "parable of God"—in that human life God has been so enacted that we have, so to say, a God-story: God is like that because God has acted like that. Having made this our primary or "root-metaphor," we can venture to use others. Dr. McFague has a fascinating list of some of the possibilities. Most of them are what she aptly calls "relational." That is, they have to do with the kinds of relationships we know in our human experience and they are applied to God as if to say "God is *like* that" yet "God is *much more* than that." She mentions: father, mother, lover, friend, savior, ruler, servant, comrade, and liberator. But she also says that there are "naturalistic" or "impersonal" images which balance the relational ones; these are found both in Scripture and in the tradition of the Church. They include rock, fortress, living water, power, sun, thunder, light, and many others. (Her discussion is on p. 15ff., of *Metaphorical Theology*, SCM Press, 1983).

I find these comments and suggestions helpful, not only because they enable us to have a wide-ranging and inclusive set of "models" for God but also because they can be a way of enriching and deepening our spiritual life as Christians. They have a certain protective aspect, too. When we think of God as "Father" we might very well give that picture patriarchal associations or predominantly male ones, with an emphasis on aggressive or coercive power. But if we qualify this Father-model by a *mother* or *friend* or *lover* picture, we are delivered from such a danger. So also the use of the more impersonal images can save us from seeing God as personal in a narrowly human sense.

A recent book by Rowan Williams, a friend and colleague on the Cambridge Faculty of Divinity, is entitled *The Truce of God* (Fontana Books 1983). He is arguing in this book that one of our contemporary problems is to be seen in the readiness to substitute what he calls "the illusions of peace" for the genuine "peace of God" which alone can provide purpose and meaning and enable us to face realistically the exigencies of our times. I quote this remarkable paragraph in which this writer speaks about the way in which in Jesus "glory and misery come together and interpret one another":

> Jesus does not achieve a theoretical solution to the problem of how 'Kingdom' and failure, future and present, hope and memory can be reconciled. He simply lives in both, the vividness of each, moment by moment, feeding the vividness of the other. He does so, the gospels suggest, because his life is given up, moment by moment, to his Father. Every moment and every experience is to be absorbed with utter serious-ness, not in bland passivity, but taken, seen, probed and responded to. This is the "obedience" of Jesus (never a very good word to describe this attitude of alert attention); and it is possible—so various bits of the New Testament suggest, and the Fourth Gospel argues explicitly—because he *sees* the Father. In the texture of all experience, joy, pain, vision, humiliation, Jesus acknowledges a single shaping love, drawing his life together into a single act of response. The world—or rather all the worlds, of grief and hope—can be sensed as given, the material given us out of which to make a whole and many-faceted offering, a gift in return. (p. 75)

Thus, he urges, the divine glory into which we are called and from which alone it is possible to achieve an existence marked by dignity and freedom, is not a matter of running away from difficulties. Neither is it a denial of the "miseries" which life's "changes and chances" inevitably can and do bring about. Rather, it is a grasp of the truth about things. For us it is to be brought to recognize that God's "glory," supremely shown in the event of Jesus Christ, has *included* within it those very miseries (now overcome and yet never erased totally) which have been shared by God with the sons and daughters of the human race—and all this ordered in a harmony whose dominant characteristic is "a single shaping love" that has the power to evoke from the creatures a "single act of response."

To pray and to witness and work, so that God's *name*—God's revealed character, God's mode of existence, and God's relationships with the creation—may be "glorified" is what Christian discipleship is about. To do this glorifying in the right way we must have the right "models" or "pictures" of God. Some critics have objected to the use of the word "picture," contending (as does Professor McFague in her excellent book) that it may imply a *literal* description of God, which is both absurd and blasphemous. If that word did suggest any such literal description, it would indeed be both absurd and blasphemous; but I do not think that this is necessarily the case. Pictures, excepting those made by a camera, never are literal—they can be suggestive, indicative, useful, moving, illuminating, and so forth, especially when they are, for example, painted portraits. Maybe Dr. McFague's problem arises from being an American who, like many in that country, seems to identify "picture" with photograph. However this may be, when we think of the "single shaping love" in and behind the creation—in other words, when we think about God—we are drawing upon a vast range of experiences, such as creativity, healing, gaining freedom, knowing blessedness and much else. The difficulty with so much of our God-thinking is that only *one* image has been taken as available, whereas there are others too. Perhaps an example here, once again, is the term "Father." This is given dominical status for us because it was Jesus' preferred way of speaking. Yet it cannot stand alone but must be complemented by other terms which also express relationships between God and humankind. Some of them I have already mentioned: mother with child, lover with beloved, friend with friend, liberator with those who are being freed from oppression.

I believe that we can only properly "glorify [God's] name" when we have taken all these into account. God is "towards" us not only in a paternal relationship, which may become dangerously patriarchal if taken alone; God is also towards us in a maternal fashion, in a lover's way, as a friend with a friend, as a giver of freedom to those who are in bondage. The Bible, and especially here the Old Testament, is very rich in such idiom. Without subscribing to all that zealous feminists argue, it is still possible to recognize that women can and often do feel excluded when the "Father" image is exclusively used. So also may the blacks, the poor, and persons of homosexual orientation. In order to correct such possible discomfort, we may—and indeed we must—employ other ways of indicating the divine-human relationship. Above all, we can use the event of Jesus Christ in its full humanity as a "parable of God"—for in that human existence was portrayed, enacted, and expressed the ways of God with men and women, whatever their sex, status, orientation, or race may be.

There is one other suggestion which may be useful here. We are all of us familiar with talk about God as "transcendent" (or "above all") and God as "immanent" (or "within all"). Some years ago, in a book dealing with the doctrine of the triune God, I proposed that there was a *third* way of speaking about God: that is, to see deity as "concomitant" (or "alongside"). This ties in with Whitehead's splendid words about God as "companion" and "fellow-sufferer." So far as I am aware, nobody seems to have taken up my proposal; or if it has been discussed at all, it has been dismissed as only another way of speaking of immanence. I disagree; I am convinced that it makes good sense to speak of the creative reality as not only more than the creation ("inexhaustible" or transcendent) and active within the creation and enabling because inspiring response (which is what immanence suggests) but also (and experientially of great value, in my judgement) to speak of God as *with* the creation and *with* the humans who are part of that creation.

If transcendence is stressed too much, the result may well be a portrayal of deity as aloof and remote and unconcerned. If immanence is stressed too much, the portrayal of God may be an almost pantheistic one, in which deity is merely "the soul of the world." But with an equal stress on "concomitance" or "companionship" (or even "friendship") there is a more rounded and adequate portrayal. God is more than the world, God is within the world, and God is with or alongside the world: here, perhaps, is a way in which the insight found in triunitarian thought may be given an experiential base and in consequence the "model" or "picture" of God be enriched and enlarged.

God as triune. To many people this will seem a doctrine that has long outworn its value. Or they may think that it is a bit of celestial mathematics in which *per impossible* three equals one and one equals three; and this appears absurd. It is true that orthodox defenders of the doctrine have sometimes written as if they had some extraordinary *entrée* into the inner life of God. Those who would interpret the doctrine in precise accordance with a pre-established conceptuality are quite likely to be forced to indulge in a good deal of stretching and straining, without reaching any conclusive results. For my part, I prefer to look upon the doctrine as a hint thrown out about a great mystery, without seeking to work it all out in precise philosophical concepts. Primarily, it has to do with how we may best give "God the glory." Indeed the ancient and miscalled "Anthanasian Creed" has a sentence which is suggestive in this respect: "This is the Catholic Faith," it says, "that we workship Godhead in trinity and Trinity in unity." *That we worship:* there is what logicians would call "the operational words."

How do we adore God, worship God, "give God the glory?" Part of the answer is that we do this by speaking of the great variety of God's ways of working. And if something *is* what it *does*, as I have insisted on earlier pages, then we may quite properly claim that in some fashion what God *is* is indeed what God *does* in the creative working, the revealing working, and the responsive working through which in deep religion the living God is seen. Or in the words just used, God is indeed "above" and utterly inexhaustible in the divine love and righteousness and creativity; God is indeed "within" as the inspirer of human hearts (and also of everything in the world) as these seek to say their "Amen" to divine out-going; and God is "alongside" as a companion and friend who lures us towards our truest fulfillment and accompanies us in all our efforts towards that goal. Or in still another way, the triune view of deity provides a parabolic expression for the richness of God in *all* the ways known to us, as well as in many ways which our human minds cannot fathom or understand. Thus there is validity in the old versicle and response: "Let us bless the Father, the Son and the Holy Spirit: let us praise and adore *him* forever." The imagery here is too masculine but its point is clear. We could also say "Let us bless the Creator, Revealer and Redeemer, and Responsive Inspirer: let us praise and adore that One forever." Or we could use language about mother and child, like Mother Julian of Norwich and other medieval saints who dared to speak of God as "our Mother" quite as often as "our Father." Or we could speak of the Liberator, the many acts of liberating, and the creative cooperation given to such activity. However we might phrase it, we should be indicating that our worship of God is no turning in praise to an impersonal principle, a "solitary monad," or an individual with the limitations which in our experience are usually associated with individuation.

My friend Professor Charles Hartshorne, the distinguished American philosopher and interpreter of Whiteheadian "Process Thought," to which the reader may know that I myself subscribe, once said to me something like this: "Doctrines like the Trinity and the Incarnation ought not to be taken literally but should be reverenced and used symbolically." I believe that was a profoundly true and highly suggestive remark. In fact I should wish to push it further and assert that all our theological statements are symbolic in quality. This does not deny or minimize their importance nor their relevance to (and necessity for) religious life. What it *does* do is to put them in the right kind of human discourse, thus delivering us from the absurdity of assuming that we can describe God and God's ways with the sort of precision which might be appropriate in some areas of scientific observation; *and* also saving us from the aridity of a so-called "spirituality" which is lacking any grounding in "how things really go in the world." We humans live symbolically, in terms of our symbolic representations. Why should we not recognize that in our religious faith the same holds true? The French writer Joubert once said that *"dieu defini est dieu fini."* "God too precisely defined is God over and done with." The recognition of the symbolic quality of our theological (and all our religious) speech will preserve us from any such peril.

It all comes down to the centrality of religious practice. In other words, what counts is what is usually known as "religious experience." But I wish to use that phrase more carefully than is often the case. When people talk of their religious experience, it is often assumed that they have had a vivid, consciously-realized awareness of the presence of God or of the working of God within their lives in such a manner that this presence or working of God is readily identified for what it is. In an Evangelical context this may be spoken about by saying that they have a sense of God which is so peculiarly itself that it cannot be mistaken for anything else; in more Catholic circles it may be matter of a keen awareness of the divine in sacramental worship. In any event, religious experience is sharply distinguished from all other experience.

Years ago my old teacher Leonard Hodgson in Oxford strongly urged a different view. He said that the possibility of someone's having that sort of vivid awareness was dependent largely upon the psychological and physiological "make-up" of the person in question. Some people, he noted, seem never to have anything of the sort, yet their genuine devoutness and discipleship cannot be denied. What Hodgson claimed was that for a genuine theist—a person who has come through whatever means to the conclusion that there is indeed a worshipful, dependable, trustworthy, unsurpassable reality operative in and behind the created order—*all* his or her experience is essentially religious. He said that this meant that all of it is seen and is lived in the light of that conviction. For a Christian, he also said, all of life is a matter of living in the confidence that God is the reality of Love acted out in the human life of Jesus of Nazareth and reflected throughout the creation, both in human existence with all its variety and also, in equally various ways, in the happenings which we know, the duties we assume, thea activity in which we engage, in objects of beauty, in statements of truth, in expressions of goodness, in seekings for justice . . . in *all* experience. To some there may come moments when this is vividly realized; to most of us, those moments are infrequent and perhaps never excitingly clear.

Hence when I say that what our discussion comes down to is the centrality of religious practice or of "religious experience" with its consequences, I am *not* speaking only of experiences of a definitively conscious presence or action. Rather, I am speaking of the whole tenor of life, lived in the deep trust that cosmic Love is supreme and all-embracing, even if it is not always obvious. The point of our praying, "the attentive presence of God," is in our setting ourselves to concentrate on this abiding reality of God. For a Christian disciple, that is "through Jesus Christ our Lord," believing that at that point in human history there is a focal and decisive disclosure and release of the divine Love which gives us the clue or key to "the scheme of things entire."

Of course there are problems which must be faced by each of us in maintaining this conviction and engaging in Christian prayer. For example, there is the inescapable fact of evil in the world at large; there is disorder and misdirection, there is the awareness of our own human inadequacy and defection amounting to what we describe as sin; there are horrors like the Holocaust of Jews in recent years; and there is the "inhumanity" of the oppressor and tyrant. Yet with all this granted—and only a blind person or a fool could deny these things—the steady conviction that God is Love is not an impossibility for any one of us. Our praying, like our other Christian activity, can be a way in which we deepen and strengthen this conviction and give ourselves to living trustfully in the light of it. That is how we "give [God] the glory."

The Compline office, which has provided the points of departure for our several discussions in this book, is a splendid way, historically grounded and beautifully suggestive, for our coming to understand this. All Christian worship, but especially eucharistic worship, is similarly a way to such trust. Christian witness to and work in the world is "the outward and visible sign" of this profound intention. To each one it will have a different and particular character; yet what binds everything together is a response made in trust to the movement of God as Love-in-act towards us, with us, in us, and for us.

Appendix

(Taken from *The Book of Common Prayer* 1979
published by The Church Hymnal Corporation)

An Order For Compline

The Officiant begins

The Lord Almighty grant us a peaceful night and a perfect
end. *Amen.*

Officiant   Our help is in the Name of the Lord;
People   The maker of heaven and earth.

The Officiant may then say

Let us confess our sins to God.

Officiant and People

Almighty God, our heavenly Father:
We have sinned against you,
through our own fault,
in thought, and word, and deed,
and in what we have left undone.
For the sake of your Son our Lord Jesus Christ,
forgive us all our offenses;
and grant that we may serve you
in newness of life,
to the glory of your Name. Amen.

Officiant

May the Almighty God grant us forgiveness of all our sins, and the grace and comfort of the Holy Spirit. *Amen.*

The Officiant then says

> O God, make speed to save us.
People   O Lord, make haste to help us.

Officiant and People

Glory to the Father, and to the Son, and to the Holy Spirit: as it was in the beginning, is now, and will be for ever. Amen.

Except in Lent, add   Alleluia.

One or more of the following Psalms are sung or said. Other suitable selections may be substituted.

Psalm 4 *Cum invocarem*

1   Answer me when I call, O God, defender of my cause;*
    you set me free when I am hard-pressed;
    have mercy on me and hear my prayer.

2   "You mortals, how long will you dishonor my glory?*
    how long will you worship dumb idols
    and run after false gods?"

3   Know that the LORD does wonders for the faithful;*
    when I call upon the LORD, he will hear me.

4   Tremble, then, and do not sin;*
    speak to your heart in silence upon your bed.

5   Offer the appointed sacrifices*
    and put your trust in the LORD.

6   Many are saying, "Oh, that we might see better times!"*
    Lift up the light of your countenance upon us, O LORD.

7   You have put gladness in my heart,*
    more than when grain and wine and oil increase.

8   I lie down in peace; at once I fall asleep;*
    for only you, LORD, make me dwell in safety.

Psalm 31 *In te, Domine, speravi*

1   In you, O LORD, have I taken refuge;
    let me never be put to shame:*
        deliver me in your righteousness.

2   Incline your ear to me;*
    make haste to deliver me.

3   Be my strong rock, a castle to keep me safe,
    for you are my crag and my stronghold;*
        for the sake of your Name, lead me and guide me.

4   Take me out of the net that they have secretly set for me,*
    for you are my tower of strength.

5   Into your hands I commend my spirit,*
    for you have redeemed me,
    O LORD, O God of truth.

Psalm 91 *Qui habitat*

1   He who dwells in the shelter of the Most High*
    abides under the shadow of the Almighty.

2   He shall say to the LORD,
    "You are my refuge and my stronghold,*
        my God in whom I put my trust."

3   He shall deliver you from the snare of the hunter*
    and from the deadly pestilence.

4   He shall cover you with his pinions,
    and you shall find refuge under his wings;*
        his faithfulness shall be a shield and buckler.

5   You shall not be afraid of any terror by night, *
     nor of the arrow that flies by day;

6   Of the plague that stalks in the darkness, *
     nor of the sickness that lays waste at mid-day.

7   A thousand shall fall at your side
     and ten thousand at your right hand, *
         but it shall not come near you.

8   Your eyes have only to behold *
     to see the reward of the wicked.

9   Because you have made the LORD your refuge, *
     and the Most High your habitation,

10   There shall no evil happen to you, *
     neither shall any plague come near your dwelling.

11   For he shall give his angels charge over you, *
     to keep you in all your ways.

12   They shall bear you in their hands, *
     lest you dash your foot against a stone.

13   You shall tread upon the lion and adder; *
     you shall trample the young lion and the serpent
         under your feet.

14   Because he is bound to me in love,
     therefore will I deliver him; *
         I will protect him, because he knows my Name.

15   He shall call upon me, and I will answer him; *
     I am with him in trouble;
     I will rescue him and bring him to honor.

16   With long life will I satisfy him, *
     and show him my salvation.

     Psalm 134 *Ecce nunc*

1   Behold now, bless the LORD, all you servants of the LORD, *
     you that stand by night in the house of the LORD.

2   Lift up your hands in the holy place and bless the LORD; *
the LORD who made heaven and earth bless you out of Zion.

At the end of the Psalms is sung or said

Glory to the Father, and to the Son, and to the Holy Spirit: *
as it was in the beginning, is now, and will be for ever. Amen.

One of the following, or some other suitable passage of Scripture, is read

Lord, you are in the midst of us, and we are called by your
Name: Do not forsake us, O Lord our God *Jeremiah 14:9, 22*

People   Thanks be to God.

or this

Come to me, all who labor and are heavy-laden, and I will
give you rest. Take my yoke upon you, and learn from me;
for I am gentle and lowly in heart, and you will find rest for
your souls. For my yoke is easy, and my burden is light.
Matthew 11:28-30

People   Thanks be to God.

or the following

May the God of peace, who brought again from the dead our
Lord Jesus, the great shepherd of the sheep, by the blood of
the eternal covenant, equip you with everything good that you
may do his will, working in you that which is pleasing in his
sight through Jesus Christ; to whom be glory for ever and
ever. *Hebrews 13:20-21*

People   Thanks be to God.

or this

Be sober, be watchful. Your adversary the devil prowls
around like a roaring lion, seeking someone to devour.
Resist him, firm in your faith. *1 Peter 5:8-9a*

People   Thanks be to God.

A hymn suitable for the evening may be sung.

Then follows

V. Into your hands, O Lord, I commend my spirit;
R. For you have redeemed me, O Lord, O God of truth.
V. Keep us, O Lord, as the apple of your eye;
R. Hide us under the shadow of your wings.

Lord, have mercy.
Christ, have mercy.
Lord, have mercy.

Officiant and People

Our Father, who art in heaven,
  hallowed be thy Name,
  thy kingdom come,
  thy will be done,
    on earth as it is in heaven.

Give us this day our daily bread.
And forgive us our trespasses,
  as we forgive those
    who trespass against us.
And lead us not into temptation,
  but deliver us from evil.

Our Father in heaven,
  hallowed by your Name,
  your kingdom come,
  your will be done,
    on earth as in heaven.

Give us today our daily bread.
Forgive us our sins
  as we forgive those
    who sin against us.
Save us from the time of trial,
  and deliver us from evil.

Officiant   Lord, hear our prayer;
People   And let our cry come to you.
Officiant   Let us pray.

The Officiant then says one of the following Collects

Be our light in the darkness, O Lord, and in your great mercy defend us from all perils and dangers of this night; for the love of your only Son, our Savior Jesus Christ. *Amen.*

Be present, O merciful God, and protect us through the hours
of this night, so that we who are wearied by the changes and
chances of this life may rest in your eternal changelessness;
through Jesus Christ our Lord. *Amen.*

Look down, O Lord, from your heavenly throne, and
illumine this night with your celestial brightness; that by
night as by day your people may glorify your holy Name;
through Jesus Christ our Lord. *Amen.*

Visit this place, O Lord, and drive far from it all snares of the
enemy; let your holy angels dwell with us to preserve us in
peace; and let your blessing be upon us always; through Jesus
Christ our Lord. *Amen.*

A Collect for Saturdays

We give you thanks, O God, for revealing your Son Jesus
Christ to us by the light of his resurrection: Grant that as we
sing your glory at the close of this day, our joy may abound
in the morning as we celebrate the Paschal mystery; through
Jesus Christ our Lord. *Amen.*

One of the following prayers may be added

Keep watch, dear Lord, with those who work, or watch, or
weep this night, and give your angels charge over those who
sleep. Tend the sick, Lord Christ; give rest to the weary, bless
the dying, soothe the suffering, pity the afflicted, shield the
joyous; and all for your love's sake. *Amen.*

or this

O God, your unfailing providence sustains the world we live
in and the life we live: Watch over those, both night and day,
who work while others sleep, and grant that we may never
forget that our common life depends upon each other's toil;
through Jesus Christ our Lord. *Amen.*

Silence may be kept, and free intercessions and thanksgivings may be offered.

The service concludes with the Song of Simeon with this Antiphon, which is sung or said by all

Guide us waking, O Lord, and guard us sleeping; that awake we may watch with Christ, and asleep we may rest in peace.

In Easter Season, add Alleluia, alleluia, alleluia.

Lord, you now have set your servant free*
   to go in peace as you have promised;
For these eyes of mine have seen the Savior,*
   whom you have prepared for all the world to see:
A Light to enlighten the nations,*
   and the glory of your people Israel.
Glory to the Father, and to the Son, and to the Holy Spirit:*
   as it was in the beginning, is now, and will be for ever. Amen.

All repeat the Antiphon

Guide us waking, O Lord, and guard us sleeping; that awake we may watch with Christ, and asleep we may rest in peace.

In Easter Season, add Alleluia, alleluia, alleluia.

Officiant   Let us bless the Lord.
People   Thanks be to God.

The Officiant concludes

The almighty and merciful Lord, Father, Son, and Holy Spirit, bless us and keep us. *Amen.*

64408 First Printing May 1985